The World's Wittiest Wisecracks

Marks and Spencer p.l.c
PO Box 3339
Chester CH99 9QS

shop online

www.marksandspencer.com

ISBN 9780091944971
Printed in the UK

The World's Wittiest Wisecracks

ROSEMARIE JARSKI

M&S

CONTENTS

PEOPLE

BOOKS & LANGUAGE

MARRIAGE & FAMILY LIFE

COMMUNICATION

WORK & BUSINESS

HOBBIES & LEISURE

POLITICS

ARTS & ENTERTAINMENT

TRAVEL & COUNTRIES

SCIENCE & TECHNOLOGY

SOCIETY & LAW

FOOD & DRINK

FOOD & DRINK – GENERAL

'Life,' said Emerson, 'consists in what a man is thinking all day.' If that be so, then my life is nothing but a big intestine.

Henry Miller

Show me another pleasure like dinner, which comes every day and lasts an hour.

Charles-Maurice de Talleyrand

Oh, boy, dinner time! The perfect break between work and drunk.

Homer Simpson

I'm so hungry I could eat a bowl of lard with a hair in it.

Corsican Brother, *Cheech & Chong's The Corsican Brothers*

I'm so hungry I could eat the dates off a calendar.

Helen Rudge, quoting her uncle

I'm so hungry I could eat a vegetable.

Al Bundy, *Married With Children*

—You seem to have a good appetite.
—Not at all, madam, but, thank God, I am very greedy.

Fellow Diner and Anthony Trollope

He's had more hot dinners than you've had hot dinners.

Anon, on Cyril Smith, MP

He's 20 stones. For his salad, you just pour vinegar and oil on your lawn and let him graze.

Jim Bakken

—What would you like for breakfast?
—Just something light and easy to fix. How about a dear little whiskey sour?

Joe Bryan and Dorothy Parker

To open champagne at breakfast is premature, like uncovering the font at a wedding.

Pierce Synnott

I always have a boiled egg. A three-minute egg. Do you know how I time it? I bring it to the boil and then conduct the overture to *The Marriage of Figaro*. Three minutes exactly.

Sir John Barbirolli

I marmaladed a slice of toast with something of a flourish.
P.G. Wodehouse, *Stiff Upper Lip, Jeeves*

A Texas breakfast is a two-pound hunk of steak, a quart of whiskey and a hound dog. If you're wondering why you need the dog – well, somebody has to eat the steak.

Texas Bix Bender

Sex: Breakfast of Champions
Badge on the racing suit of James Hunt, champion racing driver

Yogurt is one of only three foods that taste exactly the same as they sound. The other two are goulash and squid.

Henry Beard

Peach flavour yogurt tastes best on the way back up.
Brüno Gehard, aka Sacha Baron Cohen

Ah, Wensleydale! The Mozart of cheeses.

T.S. Eliot

I hate clams. To me, they're like God's little bed-pans.
Sylvester Stallone

I am known to cross a street whenever I see an anchovy coming.
Jeffrey Steingarten

A winkle is just a bogey with a crash helmet on.

Mick Miller

Canapé: a sandwich cut into 24 pieces.

Billy Rose

Buffet: a French word that means, 'Get up and get it yourself.'

Ron Dentinger

The better a pie tastes, the worse it is for you.

Ed Howe

I never drink tap water in London, because the water here is hard, limey and tastes like it's been used to rinse false teeth.

A.A. Gill

I never drink water. I'm afraid it will become habit-forming.

W.C. Fields

I drank some boiling water because I wanted to whistle.

Mitch Hedberg

It's half past four, I think we'll have tea. Put the kettle on, Harnsworth. Oh, you've put the kettle on. It suits you.

Tony Hancock

'Spit and polish' – surely one of the worst crisp flavours ever devised.

Humphrey Lyttelton, *I'm Sorry I Haven't a Clue*

With this sauce a man might eat his father.
   Leigh Hunt, quoting the verdict of a jury of taste-testers on a new sauce

Garlic is the ketchup of intellectuals.

Anon

Hotter than hell in a heatwave.
   Gary O'Shea, eating the naga-bih jolokia, the world's hottest chilli

American Danish can be doughy, heavy, sticky, tasting of prunes and is usually wrapped in cellophane. Danish Danish is light, crisp, buttery and often tastes of marzipan or raisins; it is seldom wrapped in anything but loving care.

R.W. Apple, Jr.

—What is Osama Bin Laden's favourite dessert?
—Terrormisu.

Popbitch.com

As a boy, I was seduced by the honeycomb centre of a Crunchie. I'm sure I wasn't alone in trying to make a deep hole in the honeycomb with my tongue, before the chocolate collapsed around it.

Simon Hopkinson, *Roast Chicken and Other Stories*

Liquorice is the liver of candy.

Michael O'Donoghue

Fry's Turkish Delight…a refrigerated human organ dipped in chocolate.

Charlie Brooker

Tinned soups, unless you happen to like the taste of tin, are universally displeasing.

Elizabeth David

Rightly thought of there is poetry in peaches, even when they are canned.

Harvey Granville Barker

Raspberries are best not washed. After all, one must have faith in something.

Ann Batchelder

—What's red and sits in a corner?
—A naughty strawberry.

Alan Davies, *QI*

Kiwi: a Draylon-covered tasteless fruit.
Mike Barfield, *Dictionary for our Time*

Jerusalem artichokes…are none the worse for not being artichokes and having nothing at all to do with Jerusalem.

Jane Grigson

The French'll eat anything. Over here, My Little Pony is a toy; over there, it's a starter.

Paul Merton, *Room 101*

Whilst in Normandy last summer, I found Bisto gravy powder in a hardware shop on the same shelf as colouring for tile grout.

M.J.J. Tanner

I visited a supermarket in southern Italy, where I found Bird's Custard on shelves reserved for pet foods.

I.S. Harrison

Somewhere lives a bad Cajun cook, just as somewhere must live one last ivory-billed woodpecker. For me, I don't expect ever to encounter either one.

William Least Heat-Moon

—Why is parsley like pubic hair?
—You push it aside and keep eating.

Anon

—Is it true that the Chinese will eat anything with four legs, unless it's a table?
—Yes. And anything with wings, unless it's a plane.

Andrew Purvis and Xu Ying Jie

The story about the Indian and the Cantonese confronted by a creature from outer space: the Indian falls to his knees and begins to worship it, while the Chinese searches his memory for a suitable recipe.

Paul Lévy, *Out to Lunch*

Some of the food looks good enough to eat.

Paul Merton, in India

Photographs fade, bric-a-brac gets lost, busts of Wagner get broken, but once you absorb a Bayreuth-restaurant meal, it is your possession and your property until the time comes to embalm the rest of you.

Mark Twain, dining in Germany

I feel like a bus on a wet day: full up inside.

Monica Nash, quoting an acquaintance

Always get up from the table feeling as if you could still eat a penny bun.

Joyce Grenfell and Hugh Casson, quoting 'Nanny'

COOKING

I miss my wife's cooking – as often as I can.

Henny Youngman

It took her the first 3 months of married life to discover you can't open an egg with a can opener.

Joey Adams

She has the only dining room with a garbage disposal for a centrepiece.

Bob Hope

My wife can't cook at all. She made chocolate mousse. An antler got stuck in my throat.

Rodney Dangerfield

She loves to make soup – especially 'cream of yesterday'.

Milton Berle

Hey, I stuck that in the microwave, pressed 'power', pressed 'time', pressed 'start', and this is the thanks I get?

Roseanne Conner, *Roseanne*

—This hot chocolate you made…tastes like some warm water that has had a brown crayon dipped in it.
—[*sips it*] You're right. I'll go put in another crayon.

Lucy and Linus van Pelt, *Peanuts*

The husband that uncomplainingly eats what's set before him may live more peacefully, but not as long.

Kin Hubbard

I tried boiling pig's feet once, but I couldn't get the pig to stand still.
Groucho Marx

I'm an all right cook. It depends on how much I want to sleep with you, really.

Benjamin Zephaniah

Here, taste my tuna casserole and tell me if I put in too much
hot fudge.

Larry Lipton, *Manhattan Murder Mystery*

I have enough fruitcakes in my freezer to enlarge my patio.

Erma Bombeck

Mammy's cakes are so heavy the post office won't take them.

Ernest Matthew Mickler

All you used to give me was TV dinners or convenience food…
If you'd been in charge of the Last Supper, it would have been a
takeaway.

Rodney Trotter, to Del Boy, *Only Fools and Horses*

Who bothers to cook TV dinners? I suck them frozen.

Woody Allen

I don't even butter my bread; I consider that cooking.

Katherine Cebrian

Cook book: a collection of recipes arranged in such a fashion that
the cook must turn the page just after the point where a thick paste
of flour, water and lard is mixed by hand.

Henry Beard

Skid Road Stroganoff… Add the flour, salt, paprika and
mushrooms, stir, and let it cook five minutes while you light a
cigarette and stare sullenly at the sink.

Peg Bracken

My favourite recipe: Warm up car. Let stand for an hour next to
restaurant.

Margery Eliscu

Chef: any cook who swears in French.

Henry Beard

A lot of chefs stick a banana up a duck and call themselves
geniuses.

Sanche de Gramont

—What's the difference between Gordon Ramsay and a cross country run?
—One is a pant in the country...

Popbitch.com

I'm not a smarmy arse. I don't think you should walk into the dining room and grace tables, standing there like some starched stiff erection, gawping at customers and asking how the food was.

Gordon Ramsay

If you give Heston Blumenthal a human brain he might poach it lightly in a reduction of 1978 Cornas and top it with a mortarboard made of liquorice.

Julian Barnes

Heston Blumenthal could probably make you a cloud sandwich if you asked.

Charlie Brooker

I'm sure Nigella's cooking is fantastic, but a bit wasted on me. I like toast with Dairylea, followed by Weetabix for supper.

Charles Saatchi, on his wife, Nigella Lawson
My Name is Charles Saatchi and I am an Artoholic

Was there ever anything more absurd than the cult of the stellar egg-flipper?

Will Self

I met a famous chef a few years ago: he said that while cooking was undoubtedly an art, it was the only one the products of which ended up in the sewer.

Alice Thomas Ellis

The only good vegetable is Tabasco sauce.

P.J. O'Rourke

Give peas a chance.

Tom Brokaw

—These peas are a bit big.
—They're sprouts.

Morecambe and Wise

New potatoes in their jackets or, as the Italian expression has it, in their nightshirts.

John Lanchester, *The Debt to Pleasure*

You say potato, I say vodka.

Karen Walker, *Will and Grace*

Veal is a very young beef and, like a very young girlfriend, it's cute but boring and expensive.

P.J. O'Rourke

Roast Beef, Medium, is not only a food. It is a philosophy.

Edna Ferber

Tongue – well, that's a very good thing when it ain't a woman's.

Charles Dickens, *The Pickwick Papers*

Roadkill: a roast with a lingering hint of tarmac.

Sandi Toksvig

Pâté: nothing more than a French meat loaf that's had a couple of cocktails.

Carol Cutler

There is no light so perfect as that which shines from an open fridge door at 2am.

Nigel Slater

The cold pork in the fridge was wilting at the edges; it and I exchanged looks of mutual contempt, like two women wearing the same hat in the Royal Enclosure at Ascot.

Kyril Bonfiglioli, *After You With the Pistol*

VEGETARIAN

I can smell burning flesh – and I hope to God it's human!

Morrissey, vegetarian, walking offstage in protest about a backstage barbecue

The gorilla is a strict vegetarian like the elephant and buffalo – three of the four most dangerous animals of Africa. It behooves one to walk softly with vegetarians!

Mary Hastings Bradley

If meat is murder, does that mean eggs are rape?

P.J. O'Rourke

What I always say about your salads, Annie, is that I may not enjoy eating them but I learn an awful lot about insect biology.

Reg, *Table Manners*

—I'm a vegan. Do you know what a vegan is?
—Absolutely, I never missed an episode of *Star Trek*.

Graham Perry and Vince Pinner, *Just Good Friends*

ALCOHOL

A skeleton walks into a bar and says, 'Give me a beer and a mop.'

Anon

Drunk for 1d, dead drunk for 2d, clean straw for nothing.

Sign outside a gin shop in Southwark in the 18th century

Let's get something to eat. I'm thirsty.

Nick Charles, *After the Thin Man*

I don't mind eating if it's possible to make a Martini sandwich.

Captain Benjamin 'Hawkeye' Pierce, *M*A*S*H*

—Hey, Mr Peterson, there's a cold one waiting for you.
—I know, and if she calls, I'm not here.

Woody Boyd and Norm Peterson, *Cheers*

A woman is only a woman but a frothing pint is a drink.

P.G. Wodehouse, *Pigs Have Wings*

Say when? When it's running over my knuckles.

Sir Les Patterson

Alcohol is a very necessary article... It enables Parliament to do things at eleven at night that no sane person would do at eleven in the morning.

George Bernard Shaw

Whiskey is carried into committee rooms in demijohns and carried out in demagogues.

Mark Twain

Bourbon does for me what the piece of cake did for Proust.

Walker Percy

The only time I ever said no to a drink was when I misunderstood the question.

Tom Sykes

I never worry about being driven to drink. I just worry about being driven home.

W.C. Fields

Somebody's gotta be the designated drinker.

Karen Walker, *Will and Grace*

The chief reason for drinking is the desire to behave in a certain way, and to be able to blame it on alcohol.

Mignon McLaughlin

I drink to forget I drink.

Joe E. Lewis

—What are you having?
—Not much fun.

Bartender and Dorothy Parker

I like a drink as much as the next man – unless the next man is Mel Gibson.

Ricky Gervais, Golden Globe Awards

Most of my Irish friends liked to drink to excess, on the principle that otherwise they might as well not drink at all.

Hugh Leonard

I'm an occasional drinker, the kind of guy who goes out for a beer and wakes up in Singapore with a full beard.

Raymond Chandler, *The Simple Art of Murder*

If you go to Germany and get drunk, at some point you're going to look up Hitler in the phone book.

Dave Attell

Beer is not a good cocktail-party drink, especially in a home where you don't know where the bathroom is.

Billy Carter

A good Martini should be strong enough to make your eyeballs bubble, so cold your teeth will ache, and you'll think you're hearing sleigh bells.

L.G. Shreve

You can no more keep a Martini in the refrigerator than you can keep a kiss there.

Bernard De Voto

—My father fell down the stairs with three quarts of liquor.
—Did he spill it?
—No, silly. He kept his mouth closed.

Gracie Allen and George Burns

It's like pouring diamonds into a tulip.

Advertising slogan for Dom Ruinart champagne

'He was drinking champagne out of my wife's shoe.' 'Yeah, and he wasted a good bottle of champagne. Your wife was wearing open-toed shoes.'

Larry Hagman, *Hello Darlin'*

I'll stick with gin. Champagne is just ginger ale that knows somebody.

Captain Benjamin 'Hawkeye' Pierce, *M*A*S*H*

Champagne and orange juice is a great drink. The orange improves the champagne. The champagne definitely improves the orange.

Prince Philip, Duke of Edinburgh

Gimme a bottle of Bourbon! I got a new liver and I'm breakin' it in!

Wealthy Texan, *The Simpsons*

A wonderful drink wine. Did you ever hear of a bare-footed Italian grape-crusher with athlete's foot?

W.C. Fields

By making this wine vine known to the public, I have rendered my country as great a service as if I had enabled it to pay back the national debt.

Thomas Jefferson, US president and wine importer

It's lucid, yes, but almost Episcopalian in its predictability.

Dave Barry, at a wine tasting

Being a Scotsman, I am naturally opposed to water in its undiluted state.

Alistair MacKenzie

I know bourbon gets better with age, because the older I get, the more I like it.

Booker Noe

I make it a point never to consume anything that's been aged in a radiator.

Major Charles Winchester, *M*A*S*H*

A sudden violent jolt of it has been known to stop the victim's watch, snap his suspenders and crack his glass eye right across.

Irvin S. Cobb, on moonshine corn whiskey

A toast! To my uncle, who taught me that you should always stop drinking when you can't spell your name backwards... here's to Uncle Bob!

Dan Chopin

That Scotch egg you had... I think there was more 'scotch' in it than 'egg'.

James Lipton, to Ricky Gervais

Pour him out of here!

Mae West, when W.C. Fields showed up drunk on the set of *My Little Chickadee*

Who's sober enough to drive? No one? Okay, who's drunk, but that special kind of drunk where you're a better driver because you know you're drunk?

Peter Griffin, *Family Guy*

Man, I was an embarrassing drunk. I'd get pulled over by the cops, I'd be so drunk I'd be out dancing in their lights thinking I'd made it to the next club.

Bill Hicks

I had to stop drinking because I got tired of waking up in my car driving ninety.

Richard Pryor

I've been drunk only once in my life. But that lasted for 23 years.

W.C. Fields

Anyone who stayed drunk 25 years, as I did, would have to be in trouble. Hell, I used to take two-week lunch hours.

Spencer Tracy

When doctors operated on Richard Burton three years before he died they found that his spine was coated with crystallized alcohol.

Graham Lord

Doctors don't ask the right questions to find out whether you have a drink problem. They should ask things like, 'Have you ever woken up on a plane to Turkey?'

Jenny Lecoat

An alcoholic has been...defined as a man who drinks more than his own doctor.

Alvan L. Barach

Excessive drinking of beer is likely to make the consumer fall forward; anyone overestimating his powers in regard to cider invariably falls backward.

William Pett Ridge

It takes that *je ne sais quoi* which we call sophistication for a woman to be magnificent in a drawing-room when her faculties have departed but she herself has not yet gone home.

James Thurber

I am sparkling; *you* are unusually talkative; *he* is drunk.

R.E. Kitching

In response to the question, 'What were you doing in Central Park, in Bethesda Fountain, at one in the morning, naked?' he replied, 'The backstroke.'

Leo Silver, *My Favorite Year*

Never get drunk when you're wearing a hooded sweatshirt, cos you will eventually think there's someone right behind you.

Dave Attell

Staggering home from the pub one night, Murphy passed through the cemetery, tripped into a freshly-dug grave and fell fast asleep. Next morning he awoke, looked around and said, 'Good heavens! The Day of Judgement and I'm the first up!'

Anon

Uncle Seamus, the notorious and poetic drunk… would sit down at the breakfast table the morning after a bender, drain a bottle of stout and say, 'Ah, the chill of consciousness returns.'

Molly O'Neill

The noise of the cat stamping about in the passage outside caused him exquisite discomfort.

P.G. Wodehouse, *Mr Mulliner Speaking*

I feel like the floor of a taxi cab.

Egon Spengler, *Ghostbusters*

—What hit me?
—The last Martini.

Nora and Nick Charles, *The Thin Man*

While I was asleep someone had come in and carpeted my throat.

Alan Coren

I feel like a midget with muddy feet has been walking over my tongue all night.

W.C. Fields

Be wary of strong drink. It can make you shoot at tax collectors – and miss.

Robert A. Heinlein

By the time a bartender knows what drink a man will have before he orders, there is little else about him worth knowing.

Don Marquis

—What's up, Mr Peterson?
—The warranty on my liver.

Woody Boyd and Norm Peterson, *Cheers*

He sees a psychiatrist once a week to make him stop drinking – and it works. Every Wednesday, between 5 and 6, he doesn't drink.

Joe E. Lewis

When anyone announces to you how little they drink you can be sure it's a regime they just started.

F. Scott Fitzgerald

One of life's puzzling oddities is that every centenarian has either used alcohol most of his life or has let it strictly alone.

Arnold H. Glasow

One knows where one is with a drunk, but teetotalism in an Irishman is unnatural; if it is not checked, he becomes unpredictable and repays watching.

Hugh Leonard

Don Marquis came downstairs after a month on the wagon, ambled over to the bar, and announced: 'I've conquered that goddamn willpower of mine. Gimme a double scotch.'

E.B. White

I haven't touched a drop of alcohol since the invention of the funnel.

Malachy McCourt

MONEY MATTERS

MONEY

Money is something you got to make in case you don't die.

Max Asnas

Money was invented so we could know exactly how much we owe.

Cullen Hightower

Money is what you'd get on beautifully without if only other people weren't so crazy about it.

Margaret Case Harriman

Money differs from an automobile, a mistress or cancer in being equally important to those who have it and those who do not.

J.K. Galbraith

Money is, in its effects and laws, as beautiful as roses.

Ralph Waldo Emerson

If you see a £20 note on the pavement, pick it up. Something valuable may be under it.

Anon

I don't feel like I get germs when I hold money. Money has a certain kind of amnesty... When I pass my hand over money, it becomes perfectly clean to me.

Andy Warhol

It isn't enough for you to love money – it's also necessary that money should love you.

Baron Rothschild

I can remember when you used to kiss your money goodbye. Now you don't even get a chance to blow in its ear.

Robert Orben

Right now I'd do anything for money. I'd kill somebody for money. I'd kill *you* for money. Ha ha, no, you're my friend. I'd kill you for nothing!

Chico Marx, *The Cocoanuts*

It is easy to make money. You put up the sign 'Bank' and someone walks in and hands you his money. The facade is everything.

Christina Stead

I believe that one's basic financial attitudes are – like a tendency toward fat knees – probably formed *in utero*.

Peg Bracken

When I was brought up we never talked about money because there was never enough to furnish a topic of conversation.

Mark Twain

It is physically impossible for a well-educated, intellectual, or brave man to make money the chief object of his thoughts.

John Ruskin

One should look down on money, but never lose sight of it.

André Prévot

I don't like money, but it quiets my nerves.

Joe Louis

Money is a good thing to have. It frees you from doing things you dislike. Since I dislike doing nearly everything, money is handy.

Groucho Marx

I have never been in a situation where having money made it worse.

Clinton Jones

Not having to worry about money is almost like not having to worry about dying.

Mario Puzo

If women didn't exist, all the money in the world would have no meaning.

Aristotle Onassis

—You said that money was no object!
—Oh, honey, that's just a saying, like, 'Ooh, that sounds like fun' or 'I love you'.

Grace Adler and Karen Walker, *Will and Grace*

'Extra' money is defined as that which you have in your possession just before the car breaks down.

Dick Armey

—Well, Marge, he's got all the money in the world, but there's one thing he can't buy.
—What's that, Homer?
—A dinosaur.

Homer and Marge Simpson

—Money doesn't buy happiness.
—But it upgrades despair so beautifully.

Oliver and Laurie, *Hurrah at Last*

If money doesn't make you happy, give it back!

Jules Renard

TAXATION

Taxes are a form of capital punishment.

Eddie George, governor of the Bank of England

There is no art which one government sooner learns of another than that of draining money from the pockets of the people.

Adam Smith

If you make any money, the government shoves you in the creek once a year with it in your pockets, and all that don't get wet you can keep.

Will Rogers

The taxpayer – that's someone who works for the federal government but doesn't have to take a civil service examination.

Ronald Reagan

One third of a pint of beer is tax. Not until about halfway through your pint do you stop drinking for the Government and start drinking for yourself.

Al Murray, The Pub Landlord

We've got so much taxation. I don't know of a single foreign product that enters this country untaxed except the answer to prayer.

Mark Twain

To tax and to please, no more than to love and be wise, is not given to men.

Edmund Burke

Everyone should pay tax – however rich they are.

Sir Lawrence Airey, Chairman of the Board of Inland Revenue

For several days before you put it in the mail, carry your tax return under your armpit. No Inland Revenue Service agent is going to want to spend hours poring over a sweat-stained document.

Dave Barry

I always put a dab of perfume on my tax return. Considering what they're doing to me, I might as well get them in the mood.

Bob Monkhouse

Simplified Tax Form: How much money did you make last year? Mail it in.

Stanton Delaplane

I said to my Tax Inspector, 'Have a heart!' He took it.

Bob Monkhouse

Every year, the night before he paid his taxes, my father had a ritual of watching the news. We figured it made him feel better to know that others were suffering.

Kevin Arnold, *The Wonder Years*

Do you know what Margaret Thatcher did in her first budget? Introduced VAT on yachts! It somewhat ruined my retirement.

Edward Heath

There's nothing wrong with waiting for your ship to come in, but you can be sure that if it ever does, the Receiver of Revenue will be right there to help you unload it.

David Biggs

We all hate paying taxes, but the truth of the matter is that without our tax money, many politicians would not be able to afford prostitutes.

Jimmy Kimmel

Last year I had difficulty with my income tax. I tried to take my analyst off as a business deduction. The government said it was entertainment. We compromised finally and made it a religious contribution.

Woody Allen

Last year, I deducted 10,697 cartons of cigarettes as a business expense. The tax man said: 'Don't ever let us catch you without a cigarette in
your hand.'

Dick Gregory

If you sell your soul to the Devil, do you need a receipt for tax purposes?

Mark Russell

It's true that nothing is certain but death and taxes. Sometimes I wish they came in that order.

Sam Levenson

The only difference between death and taxes is that death doesn't get worse every time Congress meets.

Will Rogers

People love the words 'tax-free'. It is like saying 'I love you'.

Diane Saunders

Next to being shot at and missed, nothing is really quite as satisfying as an income tax refund.

F.J. Raymond

Don't get excited about a tax cut. It's like a mugger giving you back your bus fare.

Arnold H. Glasow

The avoidance of taxes is the only intellectual pursuit that carries any reward.

John Maynard Keynes

The difference between tax avoidance and tax evasion is the thickness of a prison wall.

Denis Healey

Creative Accounting is a victimless crime – like tax evasion or public indecency.

Karen Walker, *Will and Grace*

You must pay taxes. But there's no law that says you gotta leave a tip.

Advertising slogan, Morgan Stanley Financial Services

Tax loopholes are like parking spaces – they all seem to disappear by the time you get there.

Joey Adams

I contact Alun Owen in Eire and ask him what the tax advantages would be if I became domiciled in Dublin. 'None,' he says. 'What you save on tax you spend on drink.'

Spike Milligan

Philosophy teaches a man that he can't take it with him; taxes teach him he can't leave it behind either.

Mignon McLaughlin

No taxation without respiration.

Steve Forbes, on the US 'death tax', a compulsory fee to pay for social care payable after death

I can't pay death duties – I do self-assessment.

Jeremy Hardy, *The News Quiz*

There's no tax on brains – the revenue would be too small.

Evan Esar

DEBT

A reminder to anyone spending like there is no tomorrow: there *is* a tomorrow.

Advertisement, Chase Manhattan Bank

I feel these days like a very large flamingo. No matter what way I turn, there is always a very large bill.

Joseph O'Connor, *The Secret World of the Irish Male*

I know at last what distinguishes man from animals: financial worries.

Jules Renard

Annual income twenty pounds, annual expenditure nineteen nineteen six, result happiness. Annual income twenty pounds, annual expenditure twenty pounds ought and six, result misery.

Charles Dickens, *David Copperfield*

Strange things happen when you're in debt. Two weeks ago, my car broke down and my phone got disconnected. I was one electric bill away from being Amish.

Tom Ryan

—We wouldn't be in this mess if you just paid the heating bill.
— I thought global warming would take care of it. Can't Al Gore do anything right?

Marge and Homer Simpson

A man properly must pay the fiddler. In my case...a whole symphony orchestra had to be subsidized.

John Barrymore

You can't put your VISA bill on your American Express card.

P.J. O'Rourke

All right, so I like spending money. But name one other extravagance!

Max Kauffmann

Thousands upon thousands are yearly brought into a state of real poverty by their great *anxiety not to be thought poor*.

William Cobbett, on keeping up appearances

When I was born, I owed twelve dollars.

George S. Kaufman

A terrible thing happened to me last week. I tried to live within my means and was picked up for vagrancy.

Robert Orben

I'm going to live within my income this year even if I have to borrow money to do it.

Mark Twain, New Year's resolution

CAPITALISM & COMMUNISM

Capitalism is the astounding belief that the most wickedest of men will do the most wickedest of things for the greatest good of everyone.

William Maynard Keynes

Capitalism is the legitimate racket of the ruling classes.

Al Capone

The trouble with the profit system has always been that it was highly unprofitable to most people.

E.B. White

The capitalist system does not guarantee that everybody will become rich, but it guarantees that anybody can become rich.

Raul R. de Sales

I am not a Capitalist, by the way; you will not find many Socialists who are not.

George Bernard Shaw

All I know is I'm not a Marxist.

Karl Marx

I ain't a communist necessarily, but I been in the red all my life.
Woody Guthrie

The capitalist system is not going to be destroyed by an outside
challenger like communism – it will be destroyed by its own internal
greed.

Molly Ivins

When it comes time to hang the capitalists they will compete with
each other to sell us the rope at a lower price.
Vladimir Ilich Lenin

In the Soviet Union, capitalism triumphed over communism. In the
United States, capitalism triumphed over democracy.
Fran Lebowitz, 1997

RECESSION

A recession is when my neighbour loses his job. A depression is
when I lose my job. A panic is when my wife loses her job.
Edgar R. Fiedler

The Great Depression, 1931, that was the year when our family ate
the piano.

James C. Wright, Jr.

The stock market has predicted nine out of the last five recessions.
Paul Samuelson

Let Wall Street have a nightmare and the whole country has to help
get them back in bed again.
Will Rogers, after the Wall Street Crash, 1929

[*urging patience after measures had been taken to promote
recovery after the Wall Street Crash of 1929*]
—You can't expect to see calves running in the field the day after
you put the bull to the cows.
—No, but I would expect to see contented cows.
Calvin Coolidge and President Herbert Hoover, 1932

Wall Street owns America. It is no longer a government of the people, by the people and for the people, but a government of Wall Street, by Wall Street and for Wall Street... Money rules.

Mary E. Lease, 1890

The complex mechanisms of the modern world depend as certainly on the faith in money as the structures of the medieval world depended on faith in God.

Lewis H. Lapham

There's a phrase we live by in America: 'In God We Trust'. It's right there where Jesus would want it: on our money.

Stephen Colbert

BANKS & BORROWING

A bank is a place that will lend you money if you can prove that you don't need it.

Bob Hope

To borrow money, big money, you have to wear your clothes in a certain way, and have about you an air of solemnity and majesty – something like the atmosphere of a Gothic cathedral.

Stephen Leacock

It is no accident that banks resemble temples, preferably Greek, and that the supplicants who come to perform the rites of deposit and withdrawal instinctively lower their voices into the registers of awe.

Lewis H. Lapham

I hesitate to deposit money in a bank. I am afraid I shall never dare to take it out again. When you go to confession and entrust your sins to the safe-keeping of the priest, do you ever come back for them?

Jean Baudrillard

There are two kinds of people in the world: those who, when taking money from a bank, carefully count it before putting it away, and those who put it away immediately, as if they can't quite believe they've actually been given it and there is a risk of their being asked for it back if they leave it in their hands for a moment longer.

Miles Kington

I think our bank is in trouble. I was about to complete a withdrawal at the cashpoint and the machine asked if I wanted to go double or quits.

The Rotarian

RICH

'Take a pencil and paper,' the teacher said, 'and write an essay with the title: "If I Were a Millionaire".' Everyone but Philip began to write furiously. 'What's the matter?' the teacher asked. 'Why don't you begin?' 'I'm waiting for my secretary.'

Bernadette Nagy

Every man nourishes within himself a secret plan for getting rich that will not work.

Grierson's Law of Minimal Self-Delusion

If I had a dollar for every time I heard, 'My God! He's covered in some sort of goo,' I'd be a rich man.

Homer Simpson

It's not the mustard that people eat that made Coleman rich, but that left on the plate!

Anon

What's the quickest way to become a millionaire? Borrow fivers off everyone you meet.

Richard Branson

Making the first million is hard, making the next hundred million is easy.

Theo Paphitis

The only thing I like about rich people is their money.

Nancy Astor

To turn $100 into $110 dollars is work. But to turn $100 million into $110 million is inevitable.

Edgar Bronfman

Sure a lot of people have money to burn. Why not? It's cheaper than gas!

Joey Adams

Those people were so rich they had a Persian rug made out of real Persians.

Henny Youngman

Once I dated a girl whose father was so rich, he had Swiss money in American banks.

Joey Adams

There are two classes of people: the have-nots and the have-yachts.

Evan Esar

If you can count your money you don't have a billion dollars.

John Paul Getty

We may see the small value God has for riches, by the people he gives them to.

Alexander Pope

Donald Trump – a man so obscenely rich he could afford to buy all the oxygen in the world, then rent it back to us at a profit if he so chose.

Charlie Brooker

He has an edifice complex. Buying buildings is his sex life.

Caroline Llewellyn, *Life Blood*

Greta Garbo earned a lot of money, and it was well invested for her. When she went shopping on Rodeo Drive, it wasn't for dresses or for jewellery; it was for Rodeo Drive.

George Cukor

You know what rich is? If Oprah ever calls you for a loan, you know you've made it.

Joan Rivers

My father somehow managed to live all his life with the gusto and philanthropy of an extremely wealthy man – without being burdened with the many complications of actually possessing any money.

Peter Ustinov

H.L. Mencken always said that every man ought to feel rich whether he had a cent or not to his name, and to that end had a habit of distributing 10-dollar bills in out-of-the-way corners of his jackets and pants pockets. 'When I accidentally come upon one of the bills,' he assured me, 'I always feel a satisfactory glow come over me and the surprise does me no end of good.' Whereupon he would lead me into the nearest drink house and set them up.

George Jean Nathan

Associate with people of cultivated tastes, and some of the culture may rub off on you. Hang around musical folk and you may, with luck, get to know Brahms from Beethoven. But keep company with the very rich and you'll end up picking up the bill.

Stanley Walker

POOR

The other day I told my wife, 'I lost my wallet, I'm very depressed.' She said, 'That makes two of you – you and the guy who found it.'

Rodney Dangerfield

I am never in during the afternoon, except when I am confined to the house by a sharp attack of penury.

Oscar Wilde

I know a fellow who's as broke as the Ten Commandments.

John Marquand

There were times my pants were so thin I could sit on a dime and tell if it was heads or tails.

Spencer Tracy

When I was a kid, my family was so poor, I had to wear my brother's hand-me-downs at the same time he was wearing them.

Redd Foxx

We were so skint when I was young that for Christmas dinner we used to have to go down to Kentucky Fried Chicken and lick other people's fingers.

Victor Lewis-Smith

Have you seen, lemons are 28 pence each? I'm having to squirt lemon washing up liquid into my gin and tonics.

Sandi Toksvig

You're not really poor until you put water on your cornflakes.

Elaine Marskon

APPEARANCE & FASHION

MAKE-UP

The most beautiful make-up of a woman is a passion. But cosmetics are easier to buy.

Yves Saint Laurent

Make-up is such a weird concept. I'll wake up in the morning and look in the mirror. 'Gee, I really don't look so good. Maybe if my eyelids were blue, I'd be more attractive.'

Cathy Ladman

I was working in a cosmetics shop. A woman came in looking for something to bring out her bright blue eyes. I gave her meat skewers.

Hattie Hayridge

Never wear yellow lipstick; never braid your eyelashes; never powder your tongue.

Miss Piggy, make-up rules

Ladies, leave your eyebrows alone. Here's how much men care about your eyebrows: do you have two of them? Okay, we're done.

Bill Maher

I did not use paint. I made myself up morally.

Eleanora Duse, actress

—I couldn't get Mimi to take off her make-up.
—I heard they tried once, and there was a whole other painting underneath it.

Lisa Robinns and Drew Carey, *The Drew Carey Show*

I have no time to put on make-up. I need that time to clean my rifle.
Henriette Mantel

—Do you have any beauty secrets?
—For attractive lips, speak words of kindness.
Interviewer and Audrey Hepburn

HAIR

When you're not blonde and thin, you come up with a personality real quick.

Kathy Najimy

A woman with her hair up always looks as if she were going some place – either to the opera or the shower.

Orson Welles

—Snow White – was she blonde or brunette?
—Only Walt Disney knows for sure.
Peter Marshall and Paul Lynde

It is great to be a blonde. With low expectations it's very easy to surprise people.

Pamela Anderson

My husband decided that blondes have more fun so he bleached his hair and asked me for a divorce.

Phyllis Diller

A man is usually bald four or five years before he knows it.
Ed Howe

Balderdash — a rapidly receding hairline.

Paul Kocak

The most expensive haircut I ever had cost a tenner. And £9 went on the search fee.

William Hague

Iain Duncan Smith and William Hague looked like two boiled eggs in blue eggcups. Their pates gleamed in unison. I gazed from the balcony in awe. If you'd stuck a few sequins on their heads they'd have looked like Dolly Parton's cleavage.

Simon Hoggart, at the Tory Party Conference

His toupee makes him look 20 years sillier.

Bill Dana

I have the insane desire to take off your toupee and butter the inside of it.

Buster Crabbe

Once a year they should have No Hairpiece Day. So everyone could see what all these baldy-headed, fake-hair jerkoffs look like.

George Carlin

Guys are lucky because they get to grow moustaches. I wish I could. It's like having a little pet for your face.

Anita Wise

When you spend weeks growing a moustache you almost fall in love with it. I had a big, thick moustache once. Everything you drink with it, you drink twice.

Bill Cosby

—Why do gay men have moustaches?
—To hide the stretch marks.

Anon

Of the Seven Dwarfs, the only one who shaved was Dopey. That should tell us something about the wisdom of shaving.

Tom Robbins, *Skinny Legs and All*

It isn't a beard until you have to decide whether to sleep with it inside or outside the duvet.

Phil Ridgway

Duvet? Who needs one if you're a real beardie? Mine's a tog factor 12.5.

Julian Heddy

FASHION & DRESS

—Why do Hell's Angels wear leather?
—Because chiffon wrinkles too easily.

Peter Marshall and Paul Lynde

Does fashion matter? Always – though not quite as much after death.

Joan Rivers

Just around the corner, in every woman's mind – is a lovely dress, a wonderful suit, or entire costume, which will make an enchanting new creature of her.

Wilhela Cushman

You could come a real cropper facing the real world after being immersed in *Vogue*.

Audrey Withers, former editor of *Vogue*

You look like a victim of designer drive-by.

Carol Muske Dukes, *Saving St Germ*

You couldn't tell if she was dressed for an opera or an operation.

Irvin S. Cobb

The prettiest dresses are worn to be taken off.

Jean Cocteau

You got to shave before you leave the house in a dress like that... and I don't mean your legs.

Don Cleveland, *The Adventures of Ford Fairlane*

I can't take you seriously if your skirt is so short I can see your tampon string.

Rachel Goodwin

Never wear anything that panics the cat.

P.J. O'Rourke

I just bought a new nightgown that would turn a monk into Jack the Ripper.

Robert J. Serling, *Wings*

—That's a beautiful nightgown.
—Yes, I spent all summer looking for a night to go with that nightgown.

Friend and Djuna Barnes

There were nine buttons on her nightgown, but she could only fascinate.

Homer Haynes

People's innermost thoughts are never as revealing as their jackets.
Fran Lebowitz

I'm trying to think of a word that describes what you're wearing... affordable!

Dame Edna Everage

—You got that entire outfit for free?
—Absolutely *au gratin*.

Landlord and Mr Glum, *The Glums*

June 14: Suit of clothes for $18 – cheaper than stealing.
Mark Twain, notebook entry

—How would you describe your style?
—I'm an intergalactic bejewelled pirate, a spindly sex stick, a he-witch scarecrow dressed by Dior.

Dan Rookwood and Russell Brand

Even on Central Avenue, not the quietest dressed street in the world, he looked about as inconspicuous as a tarantula on a slice of angel food.

Raymond Chandler, *Farewell, My Lovely*

I had a pair of jeans with studs all over them, and my friend and art critic, John Richardson, said to me: 'Ooh, you look just like a Queen Anne chair, dear.'

Nicky Haslam

I hold that gentleman to be the best dressed whose dress no one observes.

Anthony Trollope

Practical, simple, cheap and does not go out of fashion.

Fidel Castro, on battledress

Don't itch when wearing armour.

Stanislaw J. Lec

A guy goes to a fancy dress party wearing nothing but a pair of boxers. The host says, 'What the hell are you supposed to be?' The guy says, 'A premature ejaculation – I just came in my pants.'

Anon

A man wearing only bathing-shorts looks fully dressed, but a man wearing only underpants looks naked.

Miles Kington

Judge not a man by his clothes, but by his wife's clothes.

Thomas R. Dewar

If I am at home... I mostly wear leggings and an old zip-up fleece. I am really more sheep than woman.

Emma Thompson, actress

If you have a pear-shaped body, you should not wear pear-coloured clothes, or act juicy.

Demetri Martin

My clothes are addressed to women who can afford to travel with 40 suitcases.

Yves Saint Laurent

My sister has a social conscience now. She still wears her fur coat, but across the back she's embroidered a sampler that says: 'Rest in Peace.'

Julia Willis

—You paid $500 for shoes?!
—*Boots*, Todd. I'm not an idiot.

Todd Garrett and Toni Childs, *Girlfriends*

High heels were invented by a woman who had been kissed on the forehead.

Christopher Morley

—Why are so many gay men drawn to designing women's clothes?
—Because we're too scared to be plumbers.

Alex Bilmes and Alexander McQueen, fashion designer

What's in a name? A 35 per cent mark-up!

Vince Thurston, retailer, on designer names

Naomi – she's amazing – 20 years in the business and all the pressure and fame hasn't changed her a bit – she's remained a total bitch.

Brüno Gehard, aka Sacha Baron Cohen

I hate turtlenecks. Wearing a turtleneck is like being strangled by a really weak guy – all day.

Mitch Hedberg

Do you know that if you hold a shell suit up to your ear you can hear Romford?

Linda Smith, *I Think the Nurses are Stealing my Clothes*

—You know, Gracie, it takes 30 minks to make one fur coat.
—Really? How long does it take them?

George Burns and Gracie Allen

Kind-hearted Cynthia. You refused to wear fur coats taken from animals. Yes, you grew your own.

Milton Berle

I'm jealous of a woman and her purse. We men have to shove our whole lives in a little square of leather. Then we have to sit on it.

Hal Wilkerson, *Malcolm in the Middle*

When I was six I made my mother a little hat – out of her new blouse.

Lilly Daché

Top hats look like very sensible containers, suitable for holding almost everything with the exception of the human head.

George Mikes

Never try to wear a hat that has more character than you do.

Lance Morrow

If I ever get burned beyond recognition, and you can't decide if it's me or not, just put my funny fisherman's hat on my 'head'. See, it's me!

Jack Handey

All I want to know is, when are people going to stop wearing their baseball caps backwards?

Spalding Gray

When I wear a tuxedo I look like a truck driver out on a date.

Gene Kelly

I'm going to a State Dinner tonight. What do you wear to a recession?

Buffalo Bill Cody, noted by Sheldon Keller

—Do you ever wear pink?
—Only in the privacy of my own home.

Reporter and David Cameron

There will be little change in men's pockets this year.

Wall Street Journal

BEAUTY

[*in a taxi*] You look so beautiful, I can hardly keep my eyes on the meter.

Woody Allen

If you were a Broadway musical, people would be humming your face.

Elliot Garfield, *The Goodbye Girl*

She's got legs going up to her armpits – not literally; that would be hideous.

Alan Partridge

Sometimes I think this leg is the most beautiful one in the world, and sometimes the other; I suppose the truth lies somewhere in between.

Peter De Vries

The legs aren't so beautiful. I just know what to do with them.

Marlene Dietrich

All I ever seemed to get was the kind of woman who had a special dispensation from Rome to wear the thickest part of her legs below the knees.

Hugh Leonard

—Do you think a woman should be beautiful before breakfast?
—It would never occur to me to look at a woman before breakfast.

Reporter and George Sanders

But these women! If put into rough wrappers in a turnip-field, where would their beauty be?

Thomas Hardy, at a society party

Flaubert...proclaimed...that beauty was not erotic, that beautiful women were not meant to be bedded, that the only useful purpose they served was inspiring statuary.

Edmond and Jules de Goncourt

Let us leave pretty women to men without imagination.

Marcel Proust

Of course, every cat is really the most beautiful woman in the room.

E.V. Lucas

UGLY

—Models... take away all their make-up, all their expensive haircuts and those bodies, and what have you got?
—You!

Diane Chambers and Carla Tortelli, *Cheers*

I was in a beauty contest once. I not only came last, I was hit in the mouth by Miss Congeniality.

Phyllis Diller

A peeping Tom threw up on her window sill.

Jack Carter

I once took her to a masquerade party. At the stroke of midnight, I ripped off her mask and discovered I had beheaded her.

Oscar Levant, on Elsa Maxwell

By god, you'd have to go to night school to be as ugly as that.

Les Brandon, *I Didn't Know You Cared*

I know I'm ugly. My dog closes his eyes before he humps my leg.

Rodney Dangerfield

Nothing is more moving than beauty which is unaware of itself, except for ugliness which is.

Robert Mallet

COSMETIC SURGERY

Time marches on. And eventually you realize it's marching across your face.

Robert Harling

If I see something sagging, dragging or bagging, I get it sucked, tucked or plucked.

Dolly Parton

Joan Rivers passed away four years ago, but nobody told her face.

Jeffrey Ross

—How old does she look after her facelift?
—A very old twelve.

Friend and Noël Coward

You used to look your age. Now you don't even look like your species.

Greg Giraldo, to Joan Rivers

When I went for a hysterectomy I asked for a tummy tuck at the same time. I was the only woman in the hospital who wasn't sobbing when I woke up. I couldn't wait to get to the beach.

Joan Rivers

Your face has been lifted more than Bristol Palin's prom dress.

Brad Garrett, to Joan Rivers

Joan Rivers came to see me backstage on Broadway and she'd had so much work done, I couldn't tell if she liked the show.

Dame Eileen Atkins

Did you see her facelift? You may be looking at a brand new face, but you'll still be hearing the same old mouth.

Florida Evans, *Maude*

Anne Robinson's face now appears so tight and Botoxed she seems to be pushing it through the taut skin of a tambourine.

Charlie Brooker

[*doctor to female patient*] I'm not sure we should get rid of your cellulite – it may be all that's holding you together.

***Good Housekeeping* magazine, cartoon caption**

NOSE JOB

A plastic surgeon's office is the only place where no one gets offended when you pick your nose.

***MAD* magazine**

One's nose is rather like one's club or religion: there is not much really wrong with any of them, but there is something quite vulgar in wanting to change them.

Julian Fellowes

It's hard having a big nose. I can't go in the ocean. I'll be doing backstroke and someone'll shout, 'Shark!'

Rick Corso

He's the only man who can take a shower and smoke a cigar at the same time.

Wilson Mizner, on a long-nosed movie magnate

Are you eating a tomato or is that your nose?

Charlie McCarthy, to W.C. Fields

We get nose jobs all the time in the National Hockey League, and we don't even have to go to the hospital.

Brad Park, ice hockey player

Fanny Brice cut off her nose to spite her race.

Dorothy Parker, on the Jewish 'Funny Girl' who had rhinoplasty

I've always been proud of the Jews, but never so proud as tonight, because tonight I wish I had my old nose back.

Jean Carroll, actress, at a benefit for the United Jewish Appeal in May 1948 when Israel was declared a state

I spent a thousand dollars to have my nose fixed, and now my brain won't work.

Woody Allen

PEOPLE

GOOD NAME...
BAD NAME

Cheerios is a good name for a cereal but a bad name for a funeral home.

Anon

Domino's is a good name for a pizza place but a bad name for a construction company.

Tiffany Getz

Just Do It is a good slogan for Nike but a bad slogan for a suicide relief centre.

Jeff Keenan

First Impressions is a good name for a dating service but not a bungee jumping centre.

Russell Beland

Air France is a good name for an airline but a bad name for a deodorant.

Danny Bravman

Kleenex may be a good name for a tissue, but it's an excellent name for a divorce law firm.

Paul Kondis

BP is a good name for a gas company but a bad name for a honey company.

Elden Carnahan

Virgin Airways is okay as a name for an airline but not for a cigarette.

Russell Beland

Excalibur is a good name for a security company but a bad name for a tampon.

Jeff Brechlin

Nordic Track is a good name for exercise equipment but a bad name for an affirmative action program.

Larry Phillips

PEOPLE

There is a great deal of human nature in people.

Mark Twain

I am learning about people the hard way, by being one.

Ashleigh Brilliant

Three people to avoid: a man who has recently lost his luggage at an airport, a woman who has recently joined a reading group, and a child who has recently been given a how-to-be-a-magician kit.

Miles Kington

People like Coldplay and voted for the Nazis. You can't trust people.

Super Hans, *Peep Show*

I gave up trying to understand people long ago. Now I just let them try to understand me.

Snoopy, *Peanuts*

In the end we're all Jerry Springer Show guests; we just haven't been on the show.

Marilyn Manson

THERE ARE TWO KINDS OF PEOPLE IN THE WORLD...

...those who turn off a light when they leave a room, and those who don't.

Kathryn Leibovich

...those who use coasters and those who don't.

Jura Koncius

...those who brake for amber lights, and those who accelerate.

Diane White

...those who, when buying petrol, always know what the number of their pump is when asked by the cashier, and those to whom it has never occurred to look, even though this is the thousandth time they have been asked.

Miles Kington

...those who want to get to the airport two hours before flight time, and those who think they're wasting their lives if they don't leap on board as the door is closing.

Richard Reeves

...those who borrow and those who lend.

Charles Lamb

...those who laugh at their own jokes and those who don't.

Thomas Hurka

...those who hate clowns... and clowns.

D.J. MacHale, *The Quillan Games*

...cannibals and lunch.

Eric Overmyer

MEN

There's only two kinds of guys, *a prick* and *not a prick*.

Margaret Atwood

The more I study men, the more I realize that they are nothing in the world but boys grown too big to be spankable.

Jean Webster

Batteries are cheap. Who needs men?

Rebecca McLenna

Men have wonderful minds. So much is stored inside – all those sports scores and so on.

Jane Seymour

No one knows 'men' as such, any more than anyone knows 'women'… You don't know a vast crowd of identical men who roam around the place like some amorphous blob of pure, distilled masculinity. They just don't exist. Unless you count Il Divo, of course.

Julie Burchill

Men have two emotions: hungry and horny. If I don't have an erection, make me a sandwich.

Anon

The true man wants two things: danger and play. For that reason, he wants woman, as the most dangerous plaything.

Friedrich Nietzsche

Women give us solace, but if it were not for women we should never need solace.

Don Herold

WOMEN

Woman: a diet waiting to happen.

Serena Gray

Being a woman is a terribly difficult task, since it consists principally in dealing with men.

Joseph Conrad

I hate women because they always know where things are.

James Thurber

What passes for woman's intuition is often nothing more than man's transparency.

George Jean Nathan

Give a woman an inch and she'll park a car on it.

E.P.B. White

Marge, you can't keep blaming yourself. Just blame yourself once, then move on.

Homer Simpson

There are only two kinds of women – goddesses and doormats.

Pablo Picasso

Don't take for granted the English weather or the English women.

Sir Frank Worrell

They all start out as Juliets and wind up as Lady Macbeths.

Bernie Dodd, *The Country Girl*

To be a woman is something so strange, so confusing, and so complicated that only a woman could put up with it.

Søren Kierkegaard

Trust not a woman, even when dead.

Latin proverb

BATTLE OF THE SEXES

So it's *our* car, *our* flat and *our* money, but I notice it's always *her* tits. There's feminism for you.

Neil, *Viz* magazine

I'm a feminist. Not the fun kind.

Andrea Dworkin

I could never be a feminist/lesbian as there is nothing more pleasurable to me than the sight of the bottom of the washing basket on a wash day.

Mrs Merton, aka Caroline Aherne

I can't be a rose in any man's lapel.

Margaret Trudeau

Until Eve arrived, this was a man's world.

Richard Armour

Sigmund Freud asked the question: 'What is it that women want?'...But it's obvious, isn't it? They want the central heating turned up, don't they?

Al Murray, *The Pub Landlord's Book of Common Sense*

Women have very little idea of how much men hate them.

Germaine Greer, *The Female Eunuch*

How do I feel about men? With my fingers.

Cher

The only time I use women, they're either naked or dead.

Joel Silver, film producer of movies
including *Lethal Weapon* and *Die Hard*

I asked a Burmese why women, after centuries of following their men, now walk ahead. He said there were many unexploded landmines since the war.

Robert Mueller

I treat women as my equal. Of course, most women don't like to be treated like a paranoid balding Jew with contact lenses.

David Feldman

On the one hand, we'll never experience childbirth; on the other hand, we can open all our own jars.

Bruce Willis

What would happen if suddenly, magically, men could menstruate and women could not?...Men would brag about how long and how much... Sanitary supplies would be federally funded and free... Street guys would invent slang: 'He's a three-pad man'.

Gloria Steinem

Did you ever put those maxipads on adhesive side up? Makes you cranky, don't it?

Roseanne

My sister claimed sexual harassment on the job, which was a little surprising since she's a hooker.

George Miller

—Lemon, I'm impressed. You're beginning to think like a businessman.
—A business*woman*.
—I don't think that's a word.

Jack Donaghy and Liz Lemon, *30 Rock*

I love the word 'girl'. 'Gal' is pretty great, too. I don't just want to be called a 'woman'. It sounds like someone with a moustache.

Bette Midler

If the men in the room would only think how they would feel graduating with a 'spinster of arts' degree they would see how important language reform is.

Gloria Steinem, at Yale University, 1981

—Do you prefer the title 'chairperson'?
—I'd rather be a 'chairman'. They make more.

Lawyer and Dr Estelle Ramey

What is asserted by a man is an opinion; what is asserted by a woman is opinionated.

Marya Mannes

Very few men care to have the obvious pointed out to them by a woman.

Margaret Baillie Saunders

Women can do everything; men can do the rest.

Russian proverb

There will always be a battle between the sexes because men and women want different things. Men want women, and women want men.

George Burns

FRIENDS & ENEMIES

Friends are God's apology for relations.

Hugh Kingsmill

The holy passion of Friendship is of so sweet and steady and loyal and enduring a nature that it will last through a whole lifetime if not asked to lend money.

Mark Twain

Anybody can sympathize with the sufferings of a friend, but it requires a very fine nature to sympathize with a friend's success.

Oscar Wilde

I do with my friends, as I do with my books. I would have them where I can find them, but I seldom use them.

Ralph Waldo Emerson

I have 2 million friends on MySpace. That's a lot of time spent sitting in your underwear, eating Fruit Loops, clicking 'accept' over and over again.

Dane Cook

—Do you have many enemies?
—Yes, like a lot of people who can't stand idiots.

Interviewer and Bernard Blier

The French and the British are such good enemies that they can't resist being friends.

Peter Ustinov

One should forgive one's enemies, but not before they are hanged.

Heinrich Heine

BOOKS & LANGUAGE

LANGUAGES

Two sheep in a field. One turns to the other and says: 'Moo'. The other sheep says: 'What are you on about?' The first sheep says: 'I'm learning a foreign language.'

Anon

'Meow' means 'woof' in 'cat'.

George Carlin

A man who speaks three languages is trilingual. A man who speaks two languages is bilingual. A man who speaks only one language is English.

Claude Gagnière

Next to money, English is the leading international language.

Evan Esar

There is no such thing as 'The Queen's English'. The property has gone into the hands of a joint stock company, and we [Americans] own the bulk of the stock!

Mark Twain

French by sympathy, I am Irish by race, and the English have condemned me to speak the language of Shakespeare.

Oscar Wilde

English is a funny language. A fat chance and a slim chance are the same thing.

Jack Herbert

Life is a foreign language; all men mispronounce it.

Christopher Hampton

Saying, 'I apologise,' is the same as saying, 'I'm sorry.' Except at a funeral.

Demetri Martin

Very little thinking was ever done in English; it is not a language suited to logical thought. Instead, it's an emotive lingo beautifully adapted to concealing fallacies.

Robert A. Heinlein

Welsh is the only language you learn to be able to talk to fewer people.

A.A. Gill

The Romans would never have found time to conquer the world if they had been obliged first to learn Latin.

Heinrich Heine

Quidquid latine dictum sit, altum viditur.
Whatever is said in Latin sounds profound.

Anon

German is a language that has the unfortunate effect on the English ear and eye of seeming to contain nothing but orders.

Sandi Toksvig

When you start a sentence in German, you have to know in the beginning what the end will be.

Otto Friedrich

Whenever the literary German dives into a sentence, that is the last you are going to see of him till he emerges on the other side of the Atlantic with his verb in his mouth.

Mark Twain

I once heard a Californian student in Heidelberg say, in one of his calmest moods, that he would rather decline two drinks than one German adjective.

Mark Twain

I did German to A-Level...and the only use I've ever found for it is reading the sides of lorries when I'm stuck on the M20.

Marian Nyman

A French politician once wrote that it was a peculiarity of the French language that in it words occur in the order in which one thinks them.

Ludwig Wittgenstein

A peculiar virtue of French is that it enables you to say nothing more formidably than any other language I know.

H.J. Laski

If the English language made any sense, lackadaisical would have something to do with a shortage of flowers.

Doug Larson

—What word is always pronounced wrong?
—'Wrong'.

Anon

You can't be happy with a woman who pronounces both *d*s in Wednesday.

Peter De Vries

WORDS

Words fascinate me. They always have. For me, browsing in a dictionary is like being turned loose in a bank.

Eddie Cantor

Did you ever open the dictionary right to the page you want? Doesn't that feel good?

George Carlin

What's the sexiest four-word sentence in the English language? It's when a Southern woman says: 'Hey, y'all, I'm drunk.'

Jeff Foxworthy

Never use a long word when a diminutive one will do.

William Safire

I'd like to see a forklift lift a crate of forks. It would be so literal.

Mitch Hedberg

Why are haemorrhoids called haemorrhoids and asteroids called asteroids? Wouldn't it make more sense if it was the other way around?

Robert Schimmel

For years, I thought *in loco parentis* meant 'My dad's an engine driver'.

Anon

'Vuja de' is that strange feeling that none of this has happened before.

George Carlin

There is no linguistic impropriety more likely to upset people than a misspelling of their name.

Dvaid Crystal

Abso-bloody-exactly!

Alan Partridge

GRAMMAR & PUNCTUATION

All the grammar that any human being ever needs...can be learned in a few weeks from a little book as thin as a Ritz-Carlton sandwich.

Stephen Leacock

Never correct a man's grammar in bed.

Dodie Meeks

If you can't hear me, it's because I'm in parentheses.

Steven Wright

She felt in italics and thought in capitals.

Henry James

A tired exclamation mark is a question mark.

Stanislaw J. Lec

Do not be afraid of the semicolon; it can be most useful.

Ernest Gowers

A colon opens its mouth wide: woe to the writer who does not fill it with something nourishing.

Karl Krasus, noted by Theodor Adorno

—You told me about this yesterday.
—I know but I left out a comma.

Lady and Groucho Marx

The older I grow, the less important the comma becomes. Let the reader catch his own breath.

Elizabeth Zwart

No steel can pierce the human heart so chillingly as a full stop at the right moment.

Isaac Babel

Etc. – a sign used to make people believe you know more than you are telling them.

Herbert V. Prochnow

All of us recognise clichés. They fall like casual dandruff on the fabric of our prose. They are weary, stale, flat and unprofitable.

James J. Kilpatrick

Adjective salad is delicious, with each element contributing its individual and unique flavour; but a purée of adjective soup tastes yecchy.

William Safire

A line of dialogue is not clear enough if you need to explain how it's said.

Elmore Leonard

'Yes,' he said succinctly.

Danielle Steel, *Toxic Bachelors*

BOOKS

Libraries are brothels for the mind. Which means that librarians are the madams, greeting punters, understanding their strange tastes and needs, and pimping their books. That's rubbish, of course, but it does wonders for the image of librarians.

Guy Browning

On another small table stood Zuleika's library. Both books were in covers of dull gold.

Max Beerbohm, *Zuleika Dobson*

I divide all readers into two classes: those who read to remember and those who read to forget.

William Lyon Phelps

Whether it is fun to go to bed with a good book depends a great deal on who's reading it.

Kenneth Patchen

—For goodness sake, all day long you've had your nose stuck in that book – why?
—I lost my bookmark.

Dick Bentley and Jimmy Edwards, *Take it From Here*

He always held that the book with the best smell was the Harrap's French and English dictionary, a book he had bought...simply for the sake of its smell.

V.S. Naipaul, *The Mystic Masseur*

Books are useless! I only ever read one book, *To Kill a Mockingbird* and it gave me absolutely no insight on how to kill mockingbirds! Sure it taught me not to judge a man by the colour of his skin...but what good does that do me?

Homer Simpson

Naomi Klein's *No Logo* stares balefully at me from the shelf... How can I take seriously a woman who criticizes the media's obsession with beauty, and yet has such artful publicity shots?

S. Atkinson

His favourite author is the guy who wrote, 'Pull tab to open.'
Gloria, *The Jewel of the Nile*

What happened to great literature? I mean, there's nothing like getting to the end of a good book and thinking to yourself, 'Ah, *there's* Wally!'
Milton Jones

In literature as in love, we are astonished at what is chosen by others.
André Maurois

There are two motives for reading a book: one, that you enjoy it; the other, that you can boast about it.
Bertrand Russell

I bored through *Middlemarch* the past week... and nearly died from the overwork.
Mark Twain

I know of no sentence that can induce such immediate and brazen lying as the one that begins: 'Have you read...'
Wilson Mizner

—Have you ever read a book that's changed your life?
—My vibrator instruction manual.
Interviewer and Kathy Lette

Grace Metalious...is one of my all time favourites. Primarily because she has the best author's picture of all author's pictures.
John Waters, on the author of *Peyton Place*

Income tax returns are the most imaginative fiction being written today.
Herman Wouk

The ideal travel book should be perhaps a little like a crime story in which you're in search of something.
Christopher Isherwood

I speed-read my daughter's Harry Potter book in 45 minutes. It's about wizards.
Glenn Baron

The smaller the ball used in the sport, the better the book. There are superb books about golf, very good books about baseball, not very many good books about basketball, and no good books on beach balls.

George Plimpton

The ideal mystery was one you would read if the end was missing.
Raymond Chandler

Mein Kampf is the fashion bible written by Austria's black sheep, Adolf. It literally translates as: 'My Flamboyance'.
Brüno Gehard, aka Sacha Baron Cohen

One trouble with developing speed-reading skills is that by the time you realise a book is boring you've already finished it.
Franklin P. Jones

DIARY

It's not a bad idea to get in the habit of writing down one's thoughts. It saves one having to bother anyone else with them.
Isabel Colegate, on keeping a diary, *The Shooting Party*

Diary-writing isn't wholly good for one… It leads to living for one's diary instead of living for the fun of living as ordinary people do.
James Agate

The life of every man is a diary in which he means to write one story, and writes another.

J.M. Barrie

I sat down once with Alan Clark…and…we worked out that the four rules for a good political diarist were the four *i's*: immediate… indiscreet… intimate… and indecipherable.

Gyles Brandreth

CRITIC

Critics are eunuchs at a gang-bang.

George Burns

Critics are people who hated Mickey Mouse when they were children – if they ever were children.

Moss Hart

A critic is a man who expects miracles.

James Huneker

I'm so terribly clever you see... I have this extraordinary ability to see, after the event, why something didn't work, and communicate it so wittily.

Critic, played by Stephen Fry, *A Bit of Fry and Laurie*

Literature is strewn with the wreckage of men who have minded beyond reason the opinions of others.

Virginia Woolf

A fly, sir, may sting a stately horse and make him wince; but one is but an insect, and the other is a horse still.

Dr Samuel Johnson

A writer, like a woman, never knows why people like him, or why people dislike him. We never know.

Isaac Bashevis Singer

I take no more notice of the wind that comes out of the mouths of critics than of the wind expelled from their backsides.

Leonardo da Vinci

A good writer is not, *per se*, a good book critic. No more so than a good drunk is automatically a good bartender.

Jim Bishop

I was so long writing my review that I never got around to reading the book.

Groucho Marx

The music critic, Huneker, could never quite make up his mind about a new symphony until he had seen the composer's mistress.

H.L. Mencken

Mr Clarkson, the wig-maker, on being asked his opinion of a great Shakespearean production, declared it to be superb. 'You couldn't see a join,' said he.

Edward H. Sothern

One of the first and most important things for a drama critic to learn is how to sleep undetected at the theatre.

William Archer

You don't so much review a play as draw up a crushing brief against it.

Edmund Wilson

One of us is obviously mistaken. Knowing the paltry little I know, I cannot believe it is me.

William Saroyan, to 15 critics who panned his play

—What's the play about?
—It's about two hours long.

Critic and Edward Albee, his customary response when questioned by a critic

There are two kinds of dramatic critics; destructive and constructive. I am a destructive. There are two kinds of guns: Krupp and pop.

George Jean Nathan

I like only destructive critics, because they force me to be on my guard and readjust my ideas. To my mind, constructive critics are just impertinent.

Peter Ustinov

A negative judgement gives you more satisfaction than praise, provided it smacks of jealousy.

Jean Baudrillard

Genuine polemics approach a book as lovingly as a cannibal spices a baby.

Walter Benjamin

Listen carefully to first criticisms made of your work. Note just what it is about your work that the critics don't like – then cultivate it. That's the only part of your work that's individual and worth keeping.

Jean Cocteau

I divide all works into two categories: those I like and those I don't. I have no other criterion.

Anton Chekhov

Time is the only critic without ambition.

John Steinbeck

MARRIAGE & FAMILY LIFE

MARRIAGE

—Marge, will you marry me?
—Why? Am I pregnant?

Homer and Marge Simpson

It's a funny thing when a man hasn't anything on earth to worry about, he goes off and gets married.

Robert Frost

Let's get this straight: I can't sleep with anyone else for the rest of my life, and if things don't work out, you get to keep half my stuff?

Bobby Slayton

To marry, just as to become a monk, means to take an absolute risk.

Paul Evdokimov

I have a raging fear of commitment. I mean, I don't even like to write in pen.

Michael Somerville

There are men who would even be afraid to commit themselves on the doctrine that castor oil is a laxative.

Camille Flammarion

If I ever marry, it will be on a sudden impulse, as a man shoots himself.

H.L. Mencken

Prostitutes believe in marriage. It provides them with most of their trade.

Suzine, *Knave* magazine

Never marry a man you wouldn't want to be divorced from.

Nora Ephron

Mother told me…'Sweetheart, settle down and marry a rich man.'
I said, 'Mom, I *am* a rich man.'

Cher

Whenever you want to marry someone, go have lunch with his
ex-wife.

Shelley Winters

Dreadful flowers bought at a garage were a perfect metaphor for
my wedding to Chris Evans: last-minute, cheap and dead within
hours.

Carol McGiffin

Women your age are more likely to get mauled at the zoo than
get married.

Jack Donaghy, *30 Rock*

They say I married my wife because her uncle left her a whole lot
of money. That's not true. I would've married her no matter who
left her the money.

Steve McFarlin

The way taxes are, you might as well marry for love.

Joe E. Lewis

I'm getting married on April 12th. My fiancé and I still haven't
decided on the year.

Wendy Liebman

I'm so glad I didn't go for the wedding dress with the beaded top;
I would've looked like an undefrosted freezer.

Vicky Hodges, *The Archers*

The bride wore her grandmother's dress. The grandmother was
freezing.

Pam Ayres, *Ayres on the Air*

—What would you like to see on your honeymoon?
—Lots of lovely ceilings.

Jonas Cord and Monica Winthrop, *The Carpetbaggers*

He promised his fiancée the world, the moon and the stars.
On their honeymoon, he took her to the planetarium.

Joey Adams

MARRIED LIFE

There's one consolation about matrimony. When you look around
you can always see somebody who did worse.

Warren H. Goldsmith

I was always deeply devoted to Rex *before* we were married and
after we were divorced. It was that little bit in between which
proved so difficult.

Elizabeth Harrison

Marriage is like a bank account. You put it in, you take it out, you
lose interest.

Irwin Corey

When a woman gets married, it's like jumping into a hole in the ice
in the middle of winter; you do it once and you remember it the
rest of your days.

Maxim Gorky

I had a patient once who dreamed she kept her husband in the deep
freeze except for mating. Lots of men feel that way.

Robert A. Johnson, psychologist

The problem with marriage is that it ends every night after making
love, and it must be rebuilt every morning before breakfast.

Gabriel García Márquez

I always take my wife morning tea in my pyjamas. But is she
grateful? No, she says she'd rather have it in a cup.

Eric Morecambe

Jane says...she's found it helps to start each new day by arriving
down at breakfast, throwing her arms in the air and announcing,
apologetically, 'It's all my fault.'

Anne Robinson

I used to annoy my first wife so much. I used to do things deliberately to annoy her, I admit that. In the mornings, I'd wake up. God, she hated that.

Bob Monkhouse

We used to think it would be nice to sleep in one another's arms, but we never could go to sleep because our weight stopped our circulations just above the elbows.

George Bernard Shaw

What is it with men and scratching? You weren't so itchy before we were married. Why are you so itchy now we are?

Andrea McLean

I realized on our first wedding anniversary that our marriage was in trouble. My husband gave me luggage. It was packed. My mother damn near suffocated.

Phyllis Diller

I honestly thought my marriage would work because me and my wife did share a sense of humour. We had to, really, because she didn't have one.

Frank Skinner

Often the difference between a successful marriage and a mediocre one consists of leaving about three or four things a day unsaid.

Harlan Miller

I sometimes feel like the beleaguered owner of a British bulldog with learning disabilities.

Caroline Bondy, on being the wife of Toby Young

My husband asked me if we have any cheese puffs. Like he can't go and lift that couch cushion up himself.

Roseanne

I got a teenage daughter and a menopausal wife. One's getting breasts, one's getting whiskers. My life is over.

Bobby Slayton

There are two kinds of marriages: where the husband quotes the wife and where the wife quotes the husband.

Clifford Odets

I've been married 38 years myself, and I don't regret a day of it. The one day of it I don't regret was August 2nd 1936. She was off visiting her ailing mother at the time.

Eddie Mayehoff, *How to Murder Your Wife*

I never mind my wife having the last word. In fact, I'm delighted when she gets to it.

Walter Matthau

Despite all the advice about how to achieve connubial bliss, a happy marriage is usually an unearned miracle.

Sloan Wilson

SINGLE LIFE

It is always incomprehensible to a man that a woman should ever refuse an offer of marriage.

Jane Austen, *Emma*

Why get married and make one man miserable when I can stay single and make thousands miserable?

Carrie P. Snow

I'm single because I was born that way.

Mae West

Being an old maid is like death by drowning, a really delightful sensation after you cease to struggle.

Edna Ferber

One of the advantages of living alone is that you don't have to wake up in the arms of a loved one.

Marion Smith

Even if I should by some awful chance find a hair upon my bread and honey – at any rate it is my own hair.

Katherine Mansfield

There's one thing worse than being alone: wishing you were.

Bob Steele

—Who famously said 'I want to be alone'?
—Is it Terry Waite?
—Terry Waite was that poor sod held captive for five years tied to a radiator!
—Well, at least he was warm.

Jim and Barbara Royle, *The Royle Family*

FAMILY LIFE

Dignity, breeding and piles of money. That's all anyone has ever wanted from a family. But all anyone gets from most families is love.

P.J. O'Rourke

I came from a big family. Four of us slept in the same bed. When we got cold, Mother threw in another brother.

Bob Hope

I have one brother, five sisters. I had to wear a tampon just to fit in.

Dane Cook

The man with six kids will always be happier than the man with six million dollars, because the man with six million dollars always wants more.

William Feather

—I had a pretty tough childhood. At the age of 5 I was left an orphan.
—That's ridiculous. What could a 5-year-old do with an orphan?

Ernie Wise and Eric Morecambe

I come from a broken home. I broke it.

Lemmy Kilmister, of heavy metal band, Motörhead

Once you've driven your drunk father to your mom's parole hearing, what else is there?

Christopher Titus, *Titus*

My ol' man was tough. He allowed no drinking in the house. I had two brothers who died of thirst.

Rodney Dangerfield

What irritates me most about my family is that they don't drink alcohol and I do. The good thing is that I view them all as potential liver-donors.

Audience Member, *The Now Show*

Family love is messy, clinging, and of an annoying and repetitive pattern, like bad wallpaper.

P.J. O'Rourke

Maynards? So much incest in that family even the bulldog's got a club foot.

Viv Stanshall

Relations never lend one any money, and won't give one credit, even for genius. They are a sort of aggravated form of the public.

Oscar Wilde

A lot of people have been tracing their family histories on the Internet. I'm no exception, and what I've discovered is that I come from a very long line of dead people.

Pat Condell, *The Store*

Do you want to trace your family tree? Run for public office.

Patricia H. Vance

GRANDPARENTS

A Jewish grandmother is watching her grandchild playing on the beach when a huge wave comes and takes him out to sea. She pleads: 'Please God, save my only grandson. I beg of you, bring him back.' And a big wave comes and washes the boy back on to the beach, good as new. She looks up to heaven and says: 'He had a hat!'

Myra Cohen

A grandparent will put a sweater on you when she is cold, feed you when she is hungry, and put you to bed when she is tired.

Erma Bombeck

My parents used to send me to spend summers with my grandparents. I hate cemeteries!

Chris Fonseca

You should have met my granny. A marvellous woman. She lived on tinned salmon, snuff and porter and never got out of bed except for funerals.

Brendan Behan

Grandchildren can be annoying. How many times can you go, 'And the cow goes moo and the pig goes oink?' It's like talking to a supermodel.

Joan Rivers

'You're more trouble than the children are' is the greatest compliment a grandparent can receive.

Gene Perret

—Grandad, why are you sitting in the garden with no trousers on?
—Well, last week I sat out here with no shirt on and I got a stiff neck. This is your Grandma's idea.

Anon

Do you ever get your arthritic grandparents and take 'em out on the lawn and drag 'em around to rake the leaves?

Harland Williams

Today I picked up Grandma at the airport. She's now at that age where she doesn't remember. So I said: 'Thanks for coming... goodbye!'

Craig Kilborn

MOTHER-IN-LAW

—Have you ever in your life been totally and completely intimidated by another person?
—Yes. My husband's mother.

Denis Ferrara and Madonna, on Guy Ritchie's mother

—What's Steve's mom like?
—Imagine Steve. In a wig. Drunk.
Carrie Bradshaw and Miranda Hobbes, *Sex and the City*

When I got married, my mother-in-law said the bride and I made a perfect couple – except for me.

George Burns

Two cannibals are having dinner. One says, 'I can't stand my mother-in-law.' The other says, 'Then just eat the rice.'

Jerry Lewis

I should, many a good day, have blown my brains out, but for the recollection that it would have given pleasure to my mother-in-law.

Lord Byron

I know a mother-in-law who sleeps with her glasses on, the better to see her son-in-law suffer in her dreams.

Ernest Coquelin

What a wonderful place to drop one's mother-in-law!
Marshal Ferdinand Foch, on seeing the Grand Canyon

—About your mother-in-law – should we embalm her, cremate her, or bury her?
—Do all three. Don't take chances.

Myron Cohen

Of all men, Adam was the happiest; he had no mother-in-law.
Paul Parfait

HOUSE & HOME

Democracy is buying a big house you can't afford with money you don't have to impress people you wish were dead.

Johnny Carson

A 30-year mortgage at his age essentially means that he's buying a coffin.

Dwight Schrute, *The Office (USA)*

—What's the top priority for a single man buying a house?
—Is it a kitchen sink that flushes?

Jimmy Carr and Sean Lock, *8 Out of 10 Cats*

Many a man who thinks to found a home discovers that he has merely opened a tavern for his friends.

Norman Douglas

The live in a beautiful little apartment overlooking the rent.

Anon

I sold my house this week. I got a pretty good price for it, but it made my landlord mad as hell.

Garry Shandling

The worst of taking a furnished house is that the articles in the rooms are saturated with the thoughts and glances of others.

Thomas Hardy

The house feels tired, even the furniture exhausted from old marital battles, the old green sofa looks like it has been awake sobbing all night.

Garrison Keillor

During his years of poverty Balzac lived in an unheated and almost unfurnished garret. On one of the bare walls the writer inscribed the words: 'Rosewood panelling with commode'; on another: 'Gobelin tapestry with Venetian mirror.' And in the place of honour over the empty fireplace: 'Picture by Raphael.'

E. Fuller

It is ridiculous to rent things if you are a gardener; it fidgets you. Even a very long lease is upsetting. I once owned a house with a 999 years lease, and it gave me an unbearable sense of being a sort of weekend guest; it hardly seemed worth while planting the hyacinths.

Beverley Nichols

We are but tenants and…shortly, the great Landlord will give us notice that our lease has expired.

Joseph Jefferson

Come live in my heart and pay no rent!

Samuel Lover

HOUSEWORK

True or false: Jeremy Irons?

Vic Reeves and Bob Mortimer, *Shooting Stars*

—Just look at the state of this place! I could write my name in the
dust on that piano.
—Ain't education a wonderful thing!

Ted Ray and Mrs Mosseltoff, the cleaner (Harold Berens)

—Mummy, where does dust come from?
—Cremated fairies.

Five-Year-Old Child and Jil Evans

—That is *the* most disgusting bathroom I have ever seen!
—Well, we tried to clean it once, but the bacteria ate our sponge.

Kate O'Brien and Lewis Kiniski, *The Drew Carey Show*

Do you know you can get Apple and Mango Toilet Duck now when
all you want to do is sluice the bog with it, not make a fruit salad.

Roger Lewis

Brave is the man who brushes the lavatory clean, but braver still
the man who cleans the lavatory brush.

Miles Kington

I call my neighbour Mrs Clean. I finally found out why her laundry
looks so much whiter than mine. She washes it.

Phyllis Diller

I am allergic to domestic goddesses. Men would prefer a woman
with a dirty mind to a clean house.

Kathy Lette

The only day I enjoyed ironing was the day I accidentally put gin in
the steam iron.

Phyllis Diller

He's fanatically tidy. Do you know, after he takes a bath he washes
the soap.

Hugh Leonard

Show me a man who lives alone and has a perpetually clean kitchen, and eight times out of nine I'll show you a man with detestable spiritual qualities.

Charles Bukowski

That kind of so-called housekeeping where they have six bottles and no corkscrew.

Mark Twain

DIY

—How many birds does it take to screw in a light bulb?
—Two. One to run around screaming, 'What do I do?' and one to shag the electrician.

DCI Gene Hunt, *Ashes To Ashes*

Did you hear about the hundred Irish carpenters? One held the screw, one held the screwdriver, and 98 turned the wall.

Jackie Hamilton

Hammer: an instrument for smashing the human thumb.

Ambrose Bierce

Having a multiplicity of screwdrivers reminds me of the old Irish saying, 'It will come in handy, even if you never use it.'

Frank P. Dilkes

The roof leaked over our bedroom. When I told my husband to take care of it, he bought me a pair of all-weather pyjamas.

Phyllis Diller

Do you remember the first time I asked you to build something and you came in the kitchen wearing nothing but a tool belt?

Tanya Branning, to her husband, *EastEnders*

Don't sleep with a drip. Call your plumber.

Sign on a plumber's van

CHEATING

If you marry a man who cheats on his wife, you'll be married to a man who cheats on his wife.

Ann Landers

—What would you do if you found a man in bed with your wife?
—I'd kick his dog and break his white stick!

Ernie Wise and Eric Morecambe

A man returns home and finds his best friend in bed with his wife. He looks at them and says to his friend: 'I have to, but *you*?'

Larry Adler

A man comes home early and finds a naked guy hiding behind the shower curtain. He says, 'What are you doing in there?' The guy says, 'Voting.'

Lou Jacobi

Bought my wife one of those new water beds. Come home
4 o'clock in the morning, there's a guy in the middle of the floor.
I said, 'Who's that?' She said, 'Lifeguard.'

Slappy White

The bed of Sir Christopher Dilke was so large that he was alleged to be able to keep his wife in one part of the bed and his mistress in another, and neither knew the other was there.

Anthony O'Reilly

—Have you been sleeping with Rose Flamsteed?
—Not a wink.

Peter De Vries

If I caught him in bed with my wife, I'd probably tuck him in.

Mike Stephenson, sports reporter, on 6ft 2" Kiwi rugby player, Paul Rauhihi, who weighs 19 stones

Adultery is much worse than homosexuality.

Margaret Thatcher

My girlfriend had sex with my agent? I thought he only took 10 per cent.

Harris T. Telemacher, *L.A. Story*

It's hard to put a glutton permanently in front of cakes without him eating two or three of them.

Francine Distel, wife of Sacha, on his womanising

All my men cheated on me... All I ever got out of marriage, except my daughter, was some jewellery and a recipe for ravioli.

Shelley Winters, on divorcing her Italian husband

Men cheat for the same reason that dogs lick their balls: because they can.

Samantha Jones, *Sex and the City*

If we have a married employee who has a girlfriend, we terminate him. He's got a lifetime contract with his wife, and if she can't trust him, how can I?

Ross Perot, when head of EDS (Electronic Data Systems)

Middle-aged couples are five times more likely to fantasize about owning a dog than dream of an extra-marital affair.

Poll for *Reader's Digest*

SEPARATION & DIVORCE

Divorce is the future tense of marriage.

Anon

Married by Elvis. Divorced by Friday.

G.M. Rouse

One minute you're newlyweds, making love on the floor of Concorde, and the next your lawyers are fighting over who gets to keep the box your dog defecates in.

Jack Donaghy, *30 Rock*

It helps to label the books.

Juan Antonio del Rosario

My first wife divorced me on grounds of incompatibility. And besides,
I think she hated me.

Oscar Levant

—What are the grounds for your divorce?
—Marriage is sufficient.

Judge and Wilson Mizner

—Oh, John, once we had something that was pure and wonderful and good. What happened to it?
—You spent it all.

Mary and John, *I'm Sorry, I'll Read That Again*

Divorce is only less painful than the need for divorce.

Jane O'Reilly, *The Girl I Left Behind*

Divorce is a system whereby two people make a mistake and one of them goes on paying for it.

Len Deighton

My wife made me a millionaire. I used to have three million.

Bobby Hull

Alimony is like putting a dime in the parking meter after they towed your car away.

Lenny Kent

My biggest regret? Not arranging a hit man to take out my ex-wife's divorce lawyer.

Pat Cash, tennis player

In our family we don't divorce our men – we *bury* 'em.

Stella Bernard, *Lord Love a Duck*

REMARRIAGE

After divorcing his first wife, Mark Thatcher has married again. And who's the lucky lady? Well, the first wife, obviously.

Clive Anderson

Many a man owes his success to his first wife and his second wife to his success.

Jim Backus

In Biblical times, a man could have as many wives as he could afford. Just like today.

Abigail Van Buren

Nigella finds it rather common to be my third wife, and would have found it more chic to be my fifth.

Charles Saatchi, *Charles Saatchi: Question*

I know a couple that got remarried. He missed two alimony payments and she repossessed him.

Bill Barner

I don't understand couples who divorce and remarry. That's like pouring milk on a bowl of cereal, tasting it, and saying: 'This milk is sour. Well, I'll put it back in the refrigerator – maybe it will be okay tomorrow.'

Larry Miller

I married William Saroyan the second time because I couldn't believe how terrible it was the first time.

**Carol Saroyan, on her remarriage
(they divorced a year later and she married Walter Matthau)**

The room was filled with people who hadn't talked to each other in years, including the bride and groom.

Dorothy Parker, on her remarriage to Alan Campbell

I planned on having one husband and seven children, but it turned out the other way around.

Lana Turner

—Can you tell me the names of your former spouses?
—What is this, a memory test?

Justice of the Peace and Elizabeth Taylor (married 8 times to 7 husbands)

Always a bride, never a bridesmaid.

Oscar Levant, on Elizabeth Taylor

I hope you've finally found the happiness you've been looking for because, quite frankly, I'm exhausted.

Melanie Cantor, matron of honour to Ulrika Jonsson at her third wedding

The others were only my wives. But you, my dear, will be my widow.

Sacha Guitry, reassuring his fifth wife, *attrib*.

COMMUNICATION

CONVERSATION

The first human statement is a scream.

Robin Skelton

There's a curious statistic I came across recently. The average married couple converse for 20 minutes every week. What do they find to talk about?

Dave Allen

—Homer, I'd like to talk to you.
—But then I won't be watching TV. You can see the bind I'm in.

Marge and Homer Simpson

If a man speaks in the heart of a forest and no woman is there to hear him, is he still wrong?

Glen Cook

A foolish man tells a woman to stop talking, but a wise man tells her that her mouth is extremely beautiful when her lips are closed.

Anon

If you want all the conversation you can handle, put a bandage on your forehead.

Bill Vaughn

I have never heard a dull story about an actor, a parrot or a Negro preacher.

Arthur Krock

Wilfred Blunt used to say that you could put ten per cent on to any story by making its leading figure a bishop.

Edward Mars

E.F. Benson's idea of a good conversation: when neither party remembers a word of what was said afterwards.

A.C. Benson

Why can't anybody in this family talk in front of me? For years I went around thinking a surprise party was being planned for me.

Billy Tate, *Soap*

I can't stand whispering. Every time a doctor whispers in the hospital, the next day there's a funeral.

Evy, *The Gingerbread Lady*

One of the best rules in conversation is never to say a thing which any of the company can reasonably wish we had rather left unsaid.

Jonathan Swift

After eating an entire bull, a mountain lion felt so good he started roaring. He kept it up until a hunter came along and shot him. The moral: when you're full of bull, keep your mouth shut.

Will Rogers

There are very few people who don't become more interesting when they stop talking.

Mary Lowry

Howl! You will feel a few million years younger.

Stanislaw J. Lec

GOSSIP

I always say, a problem shared is... gossip!

Graham Norton

Gossip is just news running ahead of itself in a red satin dress.

Liz Smith

A rabbit can't break wind round here without her knowing about it.

Brian Aldridge, *The Archers*

The story's everywhere – spreading faster than a rent boy's cheeks.

Malcolm Tucker, *The Thick Of It*

People keep telling us about their love affairs, when what we really want to know is how much money they make and how they manage on it.

Mignon McLaughlin

Men have always detested women's gossip because they suspect the truth: their measurements are being taken and compared.

Erica Jong

Men gossip less than women, but mean it.

Mignon McLaughlin

When a man tells you what people are saying about you, tell him what people are saying about him; that will immediately take his mind off your troubles.

Edgar Watson Howe

SECRETS

What is the most dangerous possession in the world? Someone else's secret.

Marjorie Bowen

I'm hoping you can keep the secret, because normally you're about as secure as a hymen in a south London comprehensive.

Jamie, *The Thick Of It*

Love, a cough, and the itch cannot be hid.

English proverb

The cat which isn't let out of the bag often becomes a skeleton in the cupboard.

Falconer Madan

—Do you have any skeletons in your cupboard?
—Dear boy, I can hardly close the door.

Interviewer and Alan Clark, MP

There are no secrets better kept than the secrets that everybody guesses.

George Bernard Shaw

An empty envelope that is sealed contains a secret.

Stanislaw J. Lec

LETTER

If you want to discover your true opinion of anybody, observe the impression made on you by the first sight of a letter from him.

Arthur Schopenhauer

I love getting mail. Just the fact that someone licked a stamp just for you is very reassuring.

Thomas Magnum, *Magnum P.I.*

A shocking thing to admit, but I begin to value my correspondents according to whether the stamps on their envelopes are cancelled or not. A handy tip... don't peel the stamp from the envelope, peel the envelope away from the stamp.

D.J. Enright

Always serve letters with a cup of tea and a footstool. Celebrate 'the reading' slowly. It is irreverent to read a letter fast.

Macrina Wiederkehr, *A Tree Full of Angels*

He'd hold a letter up to the light to see if there was a cheque inside; if not, he'd toss it into the wastebasket.

Robert N. Linscott, on William Faulkner

This is a free country. Folks have a right to send me letters, and I have a right not to read them.

William Faulkner

I would rather lay a pipeline or dig a grave than write a letter.

Edna St Vincent Millay

There ought to be a law against computers writing letters to people.

Lewis Grizzard

It is well to write love letters. There are certain things for which it is not easy to ask your mistress for face to face, like money, for instance.

Henri de Régnier

I just wish, when neither of us has written to my husband's mother, I don't feel so much worse about it than he does.

Katharine Whitehorn

Excuse me for not answering your letter sooner. I have been so busy not answering letters lately that I couldn't get around to not answering yours in time.

Groucho Marx

Never ask two questions in a business letter. The reply will discuss the one in which you are least interested and say nothing about the other.

Brian J. Weed

The post-office is a wonderful establishment! The regularity and dispatch of it! If one thinks of all that it has to do, and all that it does so well, it is really astonishing!

Jane Austen, *Emma*

—How does a funeral director sign his correspondence?
—Yours eventually.

Anon

TELEPHONE

Telephone? It's three-thirty in the blessed AM! Even the roosters are comatose!

Colonel Sherman T. Potter, *M*A*S*H*

[*on the phone*] You want to know where you can get a hold of Mrs Potter? I don't know, she's awfully ticklish.

Groucho Marx

You never know, it could be somebody important.

Queen Elizabeth II, to a woman whose mobile rang as they chatted

The telephone is a good way to talk to people without having to offer them a drink.

Fran Lebowitz

Imagine how weird phones would look if your mouth was nowhere near your ears.

Steven Wright

Having a mobile phone is the technological equivalent of lying on the bed with your legs wide open all the time.

Anon

Today the ringing of the telephone takes precedence over everything. It reaches a point of terrorism, particularly at dinnertime.

Niels Diffrient

The marvellous thing about mobile phones is that, wherever you are, whatever you are doing, you can keep them switched off so no one will bother you.

Guy Browning

Bluetooth headset users...you're not the Chief Communications Officer of the Starship *Enterprise*. You're a shoe salesman asking your mom if you can bring over your laundry.

Bill Maher

The First Law of Mobile Phone Etiquette: the volume with which an individual speaks into the phone is in inverse proportion to that individual's personal importance.

Geoffrey Horton

The Second Law of Mobile Phone Etiquette: the length of the call is in inverse proportion to the meaningful content.

Richard Polkinghorne

Never say anything on the phone that you wouldn't want your mother to hear at your trial.

Sydney Biddle Barrows

Personally, I'm waiting for Caller IQ.

Sandra Bernhard

My relationship remains stable. Just me, the boyfriend and his BlackBerry. It's a bit like having a 'To do' list as your love rival.

Julian Clary

I use phone boxes. I think that it's only me and pimps that still do... You never have to queue.

Carolyn Braby

There are worse things than getting a call for a wrong number at 4am. It could be a right number.

Doug Larson

This bloke I met texted me, and I texted him back, but then he didn't text me again till the next day. 'Sorry I didn't text you back earlier,' he said, 'but my bat died.' I said, 'Really? I didn't know you had a bat.' He said, 'I don't. I was talking about my battery.'

Chantelle Houghton, *Celebrity Big Brother 4*

Oh, how often I wished that Thomas A. Watson had laid a restraining hand on Alexander Graham Bell's arm and said to him: 'Let's not and say we did.'

Jean Mercier

By inventing the telephone, we've damaged the chances of telepathy.

Dorothy M. Richardson

PUBLIC SPEAKING

Ladies and gentlemen – and I guess that takes in most of you...

Groucho Marx

Ladies, gentlemen, and any transgendered species.

Data, *Star Trek Nemesis*

Desperately accustomed as I am to public speaking...

Noël Coward

This speech is a bit like my tee shot. I don't know where it's going.

José María Olazábal

Speeches are like babies – easy to conceive but hard to deliver.

Pat O'Malley

There are only two things more difficult than making an after-dinner speech: climbing a wall which is leaning toward you, and kissing a girl who is leaning away from you.

Winston Churchill

I have just got a new theory of eternity.

Albert Einstein, listening to a long-winded speech

The shortest distance between two jokes makes a perfect speech.

O.A. Battista

On occasions of this kind there are two speeches which I can make; one is short and one is long. The short one is 'Thank you', the long one is 'Thank you very much'. Now that I have acquainted you with the content of both speeches I see no reason for making either.

Gordon Hewart

Ian McEwan...rose to make his speech: 'Hegel said that at the age of 50 no man should speak for longer than he can make love.' He then sat down.

Steve Bird

NEWSPAPERS & JOURNALISM

—What do you do for a living?
—I work for the United Press.
—Do you do trousers?

Groucho Marx and Journalist

I call 'journalism' everything that will be less interesting tomorrow than today.

André Gide

Marmalade dropper: a news item in a morning paper which is so shocking that it causes the reader to drop their morning toast. The US equivalent was a *muffin choker*.

Susie Dent, *The Language Report*

POPE ELOPES

A marmalade dropper

Heard a report about Lindsay Lohan getting busted with coke in her car. That's a story? Call me when they find a book in her car.

Dave Attell

Read the sports section first every morning. It talks more about mankind's successes, while other parts of the paper talk about mankind's problems or failures.

Michael Milken

You ever read an article and at the bottom, it says 'continued on page 6'? I'm, like, 'Not for me! I'm done. Why don't you stop bossing me around?'

Jim Gaffigan

Lyndon B. Johnson scrutinized the daily papers like a playwright for whom each night of his life was a new opening.

Dick Goodwin

Mrs Thatcher never read a newspaper… She did not think she had the time.

Kenneth Clarke

I sometimes think our Minister doesn't believe that he exists unless he reads about himself in the paper.

Sir Humphrey Appleby, *Yes, Minister*

Lady Middleton…exerted herself to ask Mr Palmer if there was any news in the paper. 'No, none at all,' he replied, and read on.

Jane Austen, *Sense and Sensibility*

—Mr Coward, have you anything to say to *The Sun*?
—Shine!

Reporter and Noël Coward

My press relations will be minimum information given with maximum politeness.

Jacqueline Kennedy

The trouble with interviewers is that they actually *listen* to you. All your life you grapple for the other person's attention, and when you finally get it, it's alarming.

Cynthia Buchanan

I don't mind a microscope but, boy, when they use a proctoscope, that's going too far.

President Richard Nixon, on the press

CHARACTER & HUMAN NATURE

EGO

When I think of me, I smile.

Jim Ignatowski, *Taxi*

The capacity to admire others is not my most fully developed trait.

Henry Kissinger

Egotism is the anaesthetic that dulls the pain of stupidity.

Frank Leahy

We're all here for the same reason: to love me.

Barry Manilow, to fans at a concert in New York

An ego that can crack crystal at a distance of twenty feet.

John Cheever, on Yevgeny Yevtushenko

Marginally cockier than Idi Amin.

Jasper Gerard, on Piers Morgan

—You think you're God!
—I gotta model myself after someone.

Yale and Isaac Davis, *Manhattan*

Part of me suspects I'm a loser, and part of me thinks I'm God Almighty.

John Lennon

It is more fun contemplating somebody else's navel than your own.

Arthur Hoppe

I'm not like John Lennon, who thought he was the great Almighty.
I just think I'm John Lennon.

Noel Gallagher

The height of conceit: a flea, floating down the river with a hard-on, whistling for the drawbridge to open.

Anon

We go on fancying that each man is thinking of us, but he is not;
he is like us: he is thinking of himself.

Charles Reade

BORES & BOREDOM

If you have anything to tell me of importance, for God's sake begin
at the end.

Sara Jeannette Duncan

Frank, you are the ten most boring people I know.

Captain John 'Trapper' McIntyre, M*A*S*H

Listening to him is like lying in your own coffin, hearing rainwater
seep through the cracks.

Charlie Brooker

He is so dull that even ditchwater is thinking of lodging a libel
action.

Ann Treneman, on Des Browne, MP

That man is such a bore. I haven't had my hearing aid open to him
for years.

Bernard Baruch

I find that a most effective way of quelling bores is simply to say,
suddenly and irrelevantly 'Now, Singapore – does that mean
anything to you?'

Peter Ustinov

Everybody is somebody's bore.

Osbert Sitwell

ANGER & ARGUMENT

He loses his temper on Monday and doesn't find it again until Friday.

Civil Servant, on John Prescott

He's a guy who every now and then loses it so badly he needs sat nav to find his own nipples.

Jamie, *The Thick Of It*

I am righteously indignant; *you* are annoyed; *he* is making a fuss about nothing.

***New Statesman* magazine**

Never start an argument at a dinner table; the person who isn't hungry is sure to win.

Evan Esar

—I was a bit short with Pauline – bit her head off.
—She'll grow a new one.

Sharon and Dennis Rickman, *EastEnders*

There are two theories to arguing with a woman. Neither one works.

Anon

Women are repeatedly accused of taking things personally. I cannot see any other honest way of taking them.

Marya Mannes

Unlike your thighs, your argument doesn't retain water.
Jack McFarland, to Karen Walker, *Will and Grace*

—We might consider trying to reach a compromise.
—Do I look French to you ?

Francis and Otto, *Malcolm in the Middle*

She held grudges till they died of old age, then had them stuffed and mounted.

David Weber, *Field of Dishonor*

I've had a few arguments with people, but I never carry a grudge. You know why? While you're carrying a grudge, they're out dancing.

Buddy Hackett

Never pick a quarrel – even when it's ripe.

Arnold H. Glasow

Do not argue with a spouse who is packing your parachute.

Anon

—When I get mad at you, you never fight back. How do you control your anger?
—I clean the toilet bowl.
—How does that help?
—I use your toothbrush.

Husband and Wife

RIGHT & WRONG

If you're going to do something wrong, at least enjoy it.

Leo Rosten

Most of the trouble on this planet is caused by people who must be right.

William Burroughs

The more you are in the right, the more natural that everyone else should be bullied into thinking likewise.

George Orwell

It grieves me deeply to find out how frequently and how violently wrong I can be – it doesn't seem reasonable somehow.

Dorothy Parker

It infuriates me to be wrong when I know I'm right.

Molière

Always do right. This will gratify some people, and astonish the rest.

Mark Twain

If there is one thing worse than being wrong, it's being right with nobody listening.

Flo Capp

It is easier to forgive a nation for being wrong than to forgive a man for being right.

Stanislaw J. Lec

My father...never told me the difference between right and wrong; now, I think that's why I remain so greatly in his debt.

John Mortimer

People don't ever seem to realise that doing what's right's no guarantee against misfortune.

William McFee

GOOD & BAD

People are divided into the goods and the bads. The thing is not to be caught with the goods.

Mae West

Good girls go to heaven – bad girls go everywhere.

Helen Gurley Brown

On the whole, human beings want to be good, but not too good, and not quite all the time.

George Orwell

In my family, goodness is just badness before it had something to drink.

Christopher Titus, *Titus*

I knew a man who neither drank, smoked, nor rode a bicycle. Living frugally, saving his money, he died early, surrounded by greedy relatives. It was a great lesson to me.

John Barrymore

If I repent of anything, it is very likely to be my good behaviour.

Henry David Thoreau

I have always found that so-called bad people gain in one's estimation when one gets to know them better, and good people decline.

Georg Christoph Lichtenberg

To be good is noble; but to show others how to be good is nobler and no trouble.

Mark Twain

They say the good die young. Generalissimo Francisco Franco was 82.

Richard Aregood

TRUTH & LIES

Mother always said that honesty was the best policy, and money isn't everything. She was wrong about other things too.

Gerald Barzan

Yes, even I am dishonest. Not in many ways, but in some. Forty-one, I think it is.

Mark Twain

The ability to tell lies varies with the individual. For example, a short-armed fisherman isn't nearly as big a liar as a long-armed one.

Anon

Bullshit? Or bullfact?

John Oliver

Express a mean opinion of yourself occasionally; it will show your friends that you know how to tell the truth.

Ed Howe

All cruel people describe themselves as paragons of frankness.

Tennessee Williams

The only appropriate reply to the question, 'Can I be frank?' is 'Yes, if I can be Barbara.'

Fran Lebowitz

In human relations kindness and lies are worth a thousand truths.

Graham Greene

To reach the truth, the French subtract, the Germans add, and the English change the subject.

Peter Ustinov

No one ever tells the truth about fornication or cash. In these two fields, the ego is too deeply involved for truthfulness to be possible.

Malcolm Muggeridge

He sometimes told the truth – when his invention flagged.

Max Beerbohm

The truth is more important than the facts.

Frank Lloyd Wright

The secret of life is to appreciate the pleasure of being terribly, terribly deceived.

Oscar Wilde

SMELLS

I saw this nature show about how the male elk douses himself in urine to smell sweeter to the opposite sex. What a coincidence!

Jack Handey

—Eureka!
—You donna smella so good yourself!

Friend and Chico Marx

A hint of raw sourdough dough in a vat of mayonnaise that was in a trunk of a 70s car for the summer.

Sarah Silverman, sniffing Richard Christy's scrotum

—This perfume costs $400 an ounce.
—For that price it oughta smell like money.

Bob Hope and Jimmy Durante

'Where should one use perfume?' a young woman asked. 'Wherever one wants to be kissed.'

Coco Chanel

She smelled the way the Taj Mahal looks by moonlight.

Raymond Chandler, *The Little Sister*

My cologne is distilled from the bilge-water of Rupert Murdoch's yacht.

Jack Donaghy, *30 Rock*

Hay smells different to lovers and horses.

Stanislaw J. Lec

If you want to get rid of stinking odours in the kitchen, stop cooking.

Erma Bombeck

VOICE

The voice is a second face.

Gerard Bauer

Anthony Hopkins's voice is beautiful, mellifluous; when he talks it's like being dusted with deeply perfumed talcum powder.

Sally Weale

If marble could speak, it would have sounded like John Gielgud.

The Times obituary

If a swamp alligator could talk, he would sound like Tennessee Williams. His tongue seems coated with rum and molasses as it darts in and out of his mouth, licking at his moustache like a pink lizard.

Rex Reed

Everybody knows that if female genitalia could speak, it would sound exactly like Enya.

Dylan Moran

The tympanic resonance of Richard Burton's voice is so rich and overpowering that it could give an air of verse to a recipe for stewed hare.

John McPhee

His voice was intimate as the rustle of sheets.

Dorothy Parker

Mae West had a voice like a vibrating bed.

John Kobal

That wonderful voice of hers – strange, fey, mysterious, like a voice singing in the snow.

Louise Brooks, on Margaret Sullavan, actress

Any actress *with a deep voice* is always hailed by male critics for her wit, shrewdness, intellectuality – simply because she *sounds like a man*. Example, Bacall, Kate Hepburn, Marlene – all of them nice women but by no stretch of the imagination mental giants.

Kenneth Tynan

Men are attracted to a woman with a raspy voice. We think, 'Hey, maybe she's all done yelling.'

Moody McCarthy

My vocal cords are made of tweed – I give off an air of Oxford donnishness and old BBC wirelesses.

Stephen Fry

Prince Charles's vocal chords are plainly trying to strangle him. He may well become the first monarch to lose his head from the inside out.

A.A. Gill

I've been having elocution lessons. We learned to say: 'Peter Piper picked a peck of pickled pepper'. What a waste! How often does that sentence crop up in conversation?

Beryl Reid

OPTIMISM & PESSIMISM

—How's life treating you, Norm?
—Like it caught me in bed with its wife.

Ernie 'Coach' Pantusso and Norm Peterson, *Cheers*

Things are going to get a lot worse before they get worse.

Lily Tomlin

Far be it from me to rain on anybody's parade. That's my
mother's job.

Fran Fine, *The Nanny*

I'm one of the more pessimistic cats on the planet. I make Van
Gogh look like a rodeo clown.

Dennis Miller

He must have read too many of his own plays. It gets him down,
I expect.

Noël Coward, when told of Samuel Beckett's pessimism

An optimist is a man who tells you to cheer up when things are
going his way.

Evan Esar

If ever I murdered someone, it might well be an optimist.

G.K. Chesterton

I am an optimist. It does not seem too much use being anything else.

Winston Churchill

Being an optimist after you've got everything you want doesn't
count.

Kin Hubbard

Things are going well, but my blood type is still very negative.

Richard Lewis

I'm a total pessimist. It's not that the glass is half empty. Someone
stole the glass.

Joan Rivers

Samuel Beckett was walking through a London park with a friend on a glorious day and seemed, most uncharacteristically, happy. The friend said it was the kind of sunny day that made one glad to be alive. 'I wouldn't go that far,' replied Beckett.

John Heilpern

—God. How does a woman get so bitter?
—Observation.

Dedee Truitt and Lucia DeLury, *The Opposite of Sex*

She looked like something that might have occurred to Ibsen in one of his less frivolous moments.

P.G. Wodehouse, *Summer Lightning*

I don't consider myself a pessimist. I think of a pessimist as someone who is waiting for it to rain. And I feel soaked to the skin.

Leonard Cohen

I'd like to leave you with something positive, but I can't think of anything positive to say. Would you take two negatives?

Woody Allen

Then you reach the final torment: utter despair poisoned still further by a shred of hope.

Stendhal

That light we can see at the end of the tunnel... I think it's the taxman's torch.

Stu Francis

LUCK

'What are you so happy about?' a woman asked the 98-year-old man. 'I broke a mirror,' he replied. 'But that means 7 years of bad luck.' 'I know,' he said, beaming, 'Isn't it wonderful?'

Bob Monkhouse

He's very superstitious. He thinks it's unlucky to walk under a black cat.

Max Kauffmann

Luck? If the roof fell in and he was sitting in the middle of the room, everybody else would be buried and a gumdrop would drop in his mouth.

> Leo Durocher, on Dizzy Dean

The novelist was in his late forties, tall, reddish, and looked as if life had given him an endless stream of two-timing girlfriends, five-day drunks and cars with bad transmissions.

> Richard Brautigan, *Revenge of the Lawn*

If Dolly Parton had triplets, he'd be the one on the bottle.

> Bernard Manning

He is so unlucky that he runs into accidents which started to happen to somebody else.

> Don Marquis

You know it's going to be a bad day if you wake up with your water bed busted – and you ain't got a water bed.

> Jan Murray

The rabbit's foot is a more efficient lucky charm if it comes from a rabbit that's been fed four-leaf clover.

> Pierre Légaré

Depend on the rabbit's foot if you will, but remember it didn't work for the rabbit.

> R.E. Shay

HAPPINESS & SADNESS

—What has four legs and one arm?
—A happy pit bull.

> Anon

Beware of men who cry. It's true that men who cry are sensitive to and in touch with their feelings, but the only feelings they tend to be sensitive to and in touch with are their own.

> Nora Ephron

My idea of happiness is buying a piece of land large enough where I can shoot my .22 and not hit my neighbour's dog.

John Steinbeck

Happiness? A good cigar, a good meal, a good cigar and a good woman – or a bad woman; it depends on how much happiness you can handle.

George Burns

This obnoxious happiness has to end. It's just intolerable to live with.

Luke Marsden, *Big Brother 9*

If you were happy every day of your life you wouldn't be a human being. You'd be a game-show host.

Veronica Sawyer, *Heathers*

A person will be called to account on Judgement Day for every permissible thing he might have enjoyed but did not.

The Talmud

The secret to a happy life is to run out of cash and air at the same time.

Bobby Layne

You may speak of love and tenderness and passion, but real ecstasy is discovering you haven't lost your keys after all.

***The Optimist* magazine**

Never cry over spilt milk. It could've been whiskey.

Pappy Maverick, *Maverick*

Off-screen, Humphrey Bogart cried easily – Mary Philips once said that 'he cried at card tricks'.

Ann M. Sperber

There, there, don't cry. Don't make the atmosphere damp – you know how it affects your succulents.

Pat Brandon, *I Didn't Know You Cared*

I've had a good snivel...and you do feel a bit better afterwards, like a radiator that has been bled.

Julie Burchill

MANNERS & BEHAVIOUR

GENTLEMAN

Good morning, gentlemen both.
Elizabeth I, addressing a group of 18 tailors

A gentleman is someone who always takes off his hat before striking a lady.
Anon

An Australian gentleman is someone who gets out of the bath to piss in the sink.
Anon

A gentleman should know how to carve, how to play the Stock Exchange and how to spot a soft-centred chocolate at 100 yards.
Alastair Stewart, quoting his commanding officer

I always think of the Frenchman's answer when asked if a gentleman must know Greek and Latin: 'No, but he must have forgotten them.'
Oliver Wendell Holmes

There were gentlemen and there were seamen in the navy of Charles II. But the seamen were not gentlemen; and the gentlemen were not seamen.
Thomas Babington Macaulay

I may be a liar, but at least I'm a gentleman.
W.C. Fields

Make money and the whole world will conspire to call you a gentleman.
Mark Twain

LADY

I was taught three essentials for being a lady: no whisky before six, no diamonds before dinner and never go out with men in Jaguars. Believe me, it has stood me in very good stead.

Catherine Money

I was taught that a lady never bites bread, never cuts string and only ever wears white knickers.

David Morris-Marsham

One man's lady is another man's woman; sometimes, one man's lady is another man's wife.

Russell Lynes

A lady is someone whose name only appears in the newspapers three times in her life; when she is born, when she marries and when she dies.

Unidentified Correspondent to *The Times*

PUNCTUALITY

—In *Alice in Wonderland* who kept crying, 'I'm late, I'm late!'
—Alice – and her mother is sick about it.

Peter Marshall and Paul Lynde

—Hey, I'm finally here. Better late than never!
—That wouldn't be my choice.

Diane Chambers and Carla Tortelli, *Cheers*

I am a believer in punctuality though it makes me very lonely.

E.V. Lucas

I'm never on time for an appointment in England or America. In France I'm always on time because everybody else is always late; but in Spain, where nothing starts until midnight, I'm always early.

Peter Ustinov

I cannot cure myself of punctuality.

Rev. Sydney Smith

Punctuality is sacred at Buckingham Palace, but it is the height of bad manners to look at your watch while talking to someone. With a clock in every room, you don't need to.

Robert Hardman, on the 630 royal clocks

I almost had to wait.

Louis XIV

COMPLIMENTS & FLATTERY

What I should have said: Thank you.
What I did say: It's really a mousey brown, but I use Stardust Blonde No.4 and henna for body.

Anne Scott

When a man makes a woman his wife, it's the highest compliment he can pay her, and it's usually the last.

Helen Rowland

Try praising your wife – even if it does frighten her at first.

Billy Sunday

I think the world of you – and you know what condition the world is in today.

Henny Youngman

K.: You don't say many nice things to me.
M.: Mm. But I mean all the things I don't say.

Kenneth Tynan

Nowadays we are all of us so hard up, that the only pleasant things to pay *are* compliments. They're the only things we *can* pay.

Oscar Wilde

I have always thought that if I were a rich man I would employ a professional praiser.

Osbert Sitwell

Flattery is never so agreeable as to our blind side; commend a fool for his wit, or a knave for his honesty, and they will receive you into their bosoms.

Henry Fielding

The most beautiful compliment I received was when a lady ran into me on a bicycle and said, 'I'm so sorry. I didn't see you.'

Luciano Pavarotti

Try not to be one of those people who find a slight in every compliment.

Max Rothman

—Basil!
—Coming, my little piranha fish.

Sybil and Basil Fawlty, *Fawlty Towers*

INSULTS

If a man's character is to be abused, say what you will, there's nobody like a relation to do the business.

William Makepeace Thackeray

Without being unduly vulgar, my ex-husband was so far up his own ass, he could polish his own ulcers.

Hermione Gingold

You think I'm an asshole now? You should've seen me when I was drunk.

John Cougar Mellencamp

He accused me of the thing men think is the most insulting thing they can accuse you of – wanting to be married.

Nora Ephron, *Heartburn*

Hearst married a prostitute, and then gradually dragged her down to his own level.

Moorfield Storey, on William Randolph Hearst

How *Sex and the City* are we three right now? I'm Samantha, you're Charlotte, and you're the lady at home who watches it.

Jenna Maroney, *30 Rock*

What an interesting person you probably are.

Dame Edna Everage

'Ha!' I said. And I meant it to sting.

P.G. Wodehouse, *Very Good, Jeeves!*

I'd love to stop and chat to you but I'd rather have Type 2 diabetes.

Malcolm Tucker, *The Thick of It*

SPORTS

SPORTS – GENERAL

Man, I'm so bad at sports, they used to pick me after the white kids.

Caretaker (Chris Rock), *The Longest Yard*

If there's one thing the British can still do well it is run sporting events – run them but not win them, of course.

Ravi Tikoo

It is a curious fact that you can give a…man some kind of ball and he will be thoroughly content.

Judson P. Philips

I look at Colin Meads and see a great big sheep farmer who carried the rugby ball in his hands as though it was an orange pip.

Bill McClaren

My goodness, that wee ball's gone so high there'll be snow on it when it comes down.

Bill McClaren, commentating during a rugby match

Playing snooker gives you firm hands and helps to build up character. It is the ideal recreation for dedicated nuns.

Archbishop Luigi Barbarito

Snooker's not a sport really, is it? It's just standing around with a wooden stick.

Lemmy Kilmister, of heavy metal band, Motörhead

Watching gymnastics is just like paedophilia for cowards.

Frankie Boyle, *Mock the Week*

Driving a racing car is like dancing with a chainsaw.

Cale Yarborough

I'm no hod carrier but I would be laying bricks if Jonah Lomu was running at me.

Bill McClaren, on the New Zealand rugby player

Cockfighting has always been my idea of a great sport – two armed entrées battling to see who'll be dinner.

P.J. O'Rourke

To achieve anything in this game, you must be prepared to dabble on the boundary of disaster.

Stirling Moss, on motor racing

Elite sports people are a fascinating breed: they are brilliant at what they do, but they have to be stupid enough to think it matters.

Beverley Turner, wife of James Cracknell, Olympic gold medallist

Who would want to watch a sport where the slow-motion replays are actually faster than the original action?

Jasper Carrott, on crown green bowling

I wasn't a very athletic boy. I was once lapped in the long jump.

Ronnie Corbett

The New York City Marathon is the only marathon in the world where the starter's gun gets return fire.

David Letterman

Six of us collapsed on top of each other, with a rhinoceros at the bottom. To cap it all, I was overtaken by a Womble.

Peregrine Armstrong-Jones, on his London marathon run

HORSE RACING

Is it just me or does John McCririck look a bit like a Womble?

Charlie Brooker

Anybody who finds it easy to make money on the horses is probably in the dog food business.

Franklin P. Jones

The Grand National is a moment when the whole nation comes together – like the opening of a Richard Curtis movie or the manhunt for a serial killer.

Manny Bianco, *Black Books*

I went to Huntingdon and took my grandson, Jake, who is 8; he sat in my car...reading form. 'What was I going to back?' Favourites, I explained. 'I confidently expect at least four favourites to win and shall have ten four-horse accumulators at £20. Then, on the way home, we can stop and use the winnings to buy a hotel and have afternoon tea in it.'

Clement Freud

Owning a racehorse is probably the most expensive way of getting on to a racecourse for nothing.

Clement Freud

The way his horses ran could be summed up in a word. Last. He once had a horse who finished ahead of the winner of the 1942 Kentucky Derby. Unfortunately, the horse started running in the 1941 Kentucky Derby.

Groucho Marx

If Sun Pageant were human, she'd be a model on page three of *The Times*, not *The Sun* – she's got class, you see.

Mark Rimmell

French filly, Shawanda is the equine equivalent of the woman with a hat over one eye, a cigarette holder, and revolver in her stocking top.

Richard Edmondson

Trainer, Vincent O'Brien was meticulous in his attention to detail... When he thought that The Minstrel, winner of the 1977 Derby, would be upset by the noise of the Epsom crowd, he had cotton wool stuffed in the horse's ears.

Daily Telegraph

Vincent O'Brien once said that the real beauty of having Lester Piggott ride for you in the Derby was that it got him off the other fellow's horse.

John Karter

A volcano trapped in an iceberg.

Hugh McIlvanney, on Lester Piggott

I learned from Lester Piggott's great discipline. He would lock away his Yorkie bars and cigars and when he unlocked the cupboard he would take out one piece of Yorkie at a time.

Walter Swinburn, fellow jockey

That is the first time she has had 14 hands between her legs.

John Francombe, watching Sarah Ferguson, the Duchess of York, compete in a horse race marathon in Qatar

Jockey, author, broadcaster, *Sun* newspaper columnist, womaniser – the man must be scared to unzip his flies in case the next thing he touches also turns to gold.

John Anthony, on John Francombe

Had he been on the rails at Balaclava he would have kept pace with the Charge of the Light Brigade, listing the fallers in precise order and describing the riders' injuries before they hit the ground.

Hugh McIlvanney, on Peter O'Sullevan, commentator

CRICKET

The aim of English cricket is, in fact, mainly to beat Australia.

Jim Laker

I'm not interested in sport. I'm interested in cricket. I'm always surprised to find cricket books in the library in the sports section, next to football.

John Minnion

How can you tell your wife you are just popping out to play a match and then not come back for five days?

Rafael Benitez

The traditional dress of the Australian cricketer is the baggy green cap on the head and the chip on the shoulder. Both are ritualistically assumed.

Simon Barnes

Of course it's frightfully dull – that's the whole point. Any game can be exciting – football, dirt track racing, roulette... To go to cricket to be thrilled is as stupid as to go to a Chekhov play in search of melodrama.

Alexander Whitehead, *The Final Test*

The Sri Lankan batsmen found the spin bowler harder to read than *Finnegan's Wake*.

Peter Roebuck

Clive Lloyd hits him high away over mid-wicket for four, a stroke of a man knocking a thistle top off with a walking stick.

John Arlott

There was a slight interruption there for athletics.

Richie Benaud, after a streaker invaded the field at Lord's

I thought they were only allowed two bouncers in one over.

Bill Frindall, on a female streaker at Lord's

Watching the Aussies at cricket is like a porn movie: you always know what's going to happen in the end.

Mick Jagger

Merv Hughes's mincing run-up resembles someone in high heels and a panty girdle chasing after a bus.

Martin Johnson

Shane Warne is thicker than a complete set of Wisden yearbooks.

Matt Price

Why is Phil Tufnell the most popular man in the team? Is it the Manuel factor, in which the most helpless member of the cast is most affectionately identified with?

Mike Brearley

Richie Benaud has the watchfulness of a gentlemanly salamander... To see him in the flesh is to appreciate the extent to which the voice is an extension of the man.

Steve Jacobi

If I knew I was going to die today, I'd still want to hear the cricket scores.

J.H. Hardy

FOOTBALL

One perishing morning, as the sleet stretched horizontally across Liverpool's training ground, Bill Shankly glanced up at the leaden Merseyside sky and told a group of shivering players: 'It's great to be alive. The grass is green and there's a ball. What more could a man want?'

Stephen Kelly

Football is a simple game; 22 men chase a ball for 90 minutes and at the end, the Germans win.

Gary Lineker, *attrib*.

The first ninety minutes are the most important.

Bobby Robson

Why is there only one ball for 22 players? If you gave a ball to each of them, they'd stop fighting for it.

Football Widow

It's very strange, isn't it, that you can't really tell the difference between the bar and the gents at most clubs?

Peter Cook

It was a very simple team talk. All I used to say was: 'Whenever possible, give the ball to George.'

Matt Busby, on George Best, while managing Manchester United

If you aren't sure what to do with the ball, just stick it in the net and we'll discuss your options afterwards.

Bill Shankly, to a striker

I'm not giving away any secrets to Milan; if I had my way I wouldn't even tell them the time of the kick-off.

Bill Shankly

In my time at Liverpool we always said we had the best two teams in Merseyside: Liverpool, and Liverpool Reserves.

Bill Shankly

Becoming promotions consultant to Wolverhampton Wanderers is like being asked to join the *Titanic* in mid-voyage.

Rachael Heyhoe-Flint

A football team is like a piano. You need 8 men to carry it and 3 who can play the damn thing.

Bill Shankly

Can you imagine what it would be like living in London if that bunch of precious, overpaid tossers win the World Cup?

John Humphrys, on England's football squad, 2002

—What would you be if you weren't a footballer?
—A virgin!

Reporter and Peter Crouch

I can't remember anything about my first-ever goal. It was against Oldham, Andy Goram was in goal, Alan Irvine crossed it for me and we won 3–2.

Ian Wright

There are kids out there who'd chop their legs off to play football for Brighton.

Robbie Savage

Dumfries is a lovely town but it has traditionally been to football what Reykjavik is to camel racing.

Michael Gove, on the successes of Queen of the South

I went to watch Spurs at White Hart Lane last week. I stayed until the very end of the game to avoid the traffic.

Frank Skinner

It's like a toaster, the ref's shirt pocket. Every time there's a tackle, up pops a yellow card.

Kevin Keegan

I never got booked because I never made a single tackle in my career.

Gary Lineker

God must have had a big game coming up.

Inscription on a wreath at Bobby Moore's funeral

The most intelligent bit of spectator violence I ever heard of happened at a football match in Brazil. An enraged spectator drew his gun and shot the ball.

John Cohen

—You've got to say that Tony Hateley's good in the air, Bill.
—Aye, so was Douglas Bader – and he had a wooden leg.

Tommy Docherty and Bill Shankly

Tom Finney would have been great in any team, in any match and in any age...even if he had been wearing an overcoat.

Bill Shankly

I shall continue to give Luton my support. In fact, I'm wearing it at this very moment. Some people think it's just the way I walk.

Eric Morecambe

I know this is a sad occasion, but I think that Dixie would be amazed to know that even in death he could draw a bigger crowd to Goodison than Everton on a Saturday afternoon.

**Bill Shankly, Liverpool manager, at the funeral
of legendary Everton player, Dixie Dean**

GOLF

Have you ever noticed what golf spells backwards?

Al Boliska

They call it golf because all the other four-letter words were taken.

Ray Floyd

Golf is a game in which a ball – 1½ inches in diameter – is placed on a ball – 8,000 miles in diameter. The object being to hit the small ball...but not the larger.

John Cunningham

A golf ball is like a clock. Always hit it at 6 o'clock and make it go toward 12 o'clock. Just be sure you're in the same time zone.

Chi Chi Rodriguez

Imagine the ball has little legs, and chop them off.

Henry Cotton

Woodrow Wilson was a rather fidgety player who addressed the ball as if to reason with it.

Anon

Jim Furyk's swing is like an octopus falling out of a tree, or a man trying to kill a snake in a telephone booth.

David Feherty

My swing is so bad I look like a caveman killing his lunch.

Lee Trevino

I can make divots in which a small boy could get lost.

Lewis Grizzard

Golf…is not particularly a natural game. Like sword-swallowing, it has to be learned.

Brian Swarbrick

My goal is to play 72 holes someday without changing expression.

Jack Renner

The uglier a man's legs are, the better he plays golf – it's almost a law.

H.G. Wells

I can airmail the golf ball, but sometimes I don't put the right address on it.

Jim Dent

Golf tips are like aspirin. One may do you good, but if you swallow the whole bottle, you will be lucky to survive.

Harvey Penick

Keep on hitting it straight until the wee ball goes in the hole.

James Braid

—How can I get more distance on my tee shots?
—Hit it – and run backwards.

Amateur Golfer and Ken Venturi

Golf is like sex. Trying your hardest is the worst thing you can do.

Rick Reilly

I've hit more balls than Sir Elton John's chin this year, and still missed 16 cuts in a row.

David Feherty

I'm not saying my golf game went bad, but if I grew tomatoes, they'd come up sliced.

Miller Barber

—What should I take here?
—Well, sir, I recommend the 4:05 train.

Harry Vardon and Caddie

Once when I was golfing in Georgia, I hooked the ball into the swamp. I went in after it and found an alligator wearing a shirt with a picture of a little golfer on it.

Buddy Hackett

Two balls in the water. By God, I've got a good mind to jump in and make it four!

Simon Hobday

One of the advantages bowling has over golf is that you seldom lose a bowling ball.

Don Carter

At 15 we put down my bag to hunt for the ball, found the ball, lost the bag.

Lee Trevino, at Royal Birkdale

Tiger Woods hit a dangerous 3-wood approach to the green on the 18th, which runs along the Pacific at Pebble Beach. David Feherty stops him walking off and says, 'Tiger, great shot. But didn't you see that big blue thing to your left?'

Lance Barrow

I could never believe in a game where the one who hits the ball least wins.

Winston Churchill

I got down to a nine handicap. The day I became a single digit, I called my agent and said: 'You have to look harder. I shouldn't be this good at golf.'

Jason Bateman, actor

I tried for years to slow my swing. Then all of a sudden it came – like whistling.

Tony Jacklin

That shot on eight just sort of landed on the green like a snowflake.

Sam Snead

I think golf is the hardest sport to play. One day you're up on Cloud Nine, and the next day you couldn't scratch a whale's belly.

Sam Snead

Some guys get so nervous playing for their own money, the greens don't need fertilizing for a year.

Dave Hill

I am so tense at times that I can hear the bees farting.

Mick O'Loughlin

Never bet with anyone you meet on the first tee who has a deep suntan, a one-iron in his bag, and squinty eyes.

Dave Marr

You can always spot an employee who's playing golf with his boss. He's the fellow who gets a hole-in-one and says, 'Oops!'

Bob Monkhouse

Your playing partner took more strokes than an eighth-grade schoolboy with a Victoria's Secret catalogue.

David Feherty

My golfing partner couldn't hit a tiled floor with a bellyful of puke.

David Feherty

I used to play golf with a guy who cheated so badly that he once had a hole in one and wrote down zero on the scorecard.

Bob Bruce

It is as easy to lower your handicap as it is to reduce your hat size.

Henry Beard

Golf: I hate it. No wonder Hitler died in a bunker.

Alan Coren, noted by Sandi Toksvig

That putt was so fast I don't think they mow the greens, I think they bikini wax 'em!

Gary McCord, at The Masters in Augusta

Some players would complain if they had to play on Dolly Parton's bedspread.

Jimmy Demaret

You can't trust anybody these days.

Peter Allis, after a player made the sign of the cross before playing a bunker shot only to miss the ball completely

If every golfer in the world, male and female, were laid end to end, I, for one, would leave them there.

Michael Parkinson

BOXING

Boxing is...a celebration of the lost religion of masculinity all the more trenchant for its being lost.

Joyce Carol Oates

I'm so fast I could hit you before God gets the news.

Muhammad Ali

Not only do I knock 'em out, I pick the round.

Muhammad Ali

Everybody's got a plan – until he gets hit.

Mike Tyson

I'll never forget my first fight. All of a sudden I found someone I knew in the fourth row. It was me.

Henny Youngman

Sure the fight was fixed. I fixed it with a right hand.

George Foreman

The stubble on his chin even hurts you.

Glenn McCrory, on Mike Tyson

It's gonna be a thrilla, a chilla, and a killa, when I get the gorilla in Manila.

Muhammad Ali, on Joe Frazier

If only one of them would just say, 'I'm sorry.'

Joe Ancis, watching a boxing match on TV

The last time Frank Bruno fought Mike Tyson I had a bet on Frank, but I also had a bet on Elvis Presley sitting at ringside.

John H. Stracey

—Are you going to retire from boxing?
—It depends – just throw a punch at me.

Reporter and Lennox Lewis

—Prizefighter Stanley Ketchel's been shot!
—Tell 'em to start counting ten over him, and he'll get up.

Friend and Wilson Mizner

TENNIS

—What time does Sean Connery get to Wimbledon?
—Tennish.

Popbitch.com

If God had wanted me to play tennis, He would have given me less leg and more room to store the ball.

Erma Bombeck

Tennis: a middle-class version of professional wrestling.

John Ralston Saul

I always thought Tim Henman's racket had more personality than he did.

Edwina Currie

Like a Volvo, Björn Borg is rugged, has good after-sales service, and is very dull.

Clive James

—Who is the best doubles team in history?
—John McEnroe and anyone.

**Reporter and Peter Fleming, who partnered
McEnroe to 7 Grand Slam doubles titles**

Tennis should be played only in the long grass in the meadows –
and in the nude.

George Bernard Shaw

It's not really a shorter skirt, I just have longer legs.

Anna Kournikova

Female tennis players must be able to control their grunting. Can't
they just try and pretend that their parents are in the next room?

Jeremy Hardy, *The News Quiz*

—What's the key to the final?
—Win the last point.

Reporter and Jim Courier

WORK & BUSINESS

WORK

—What's the difference between your wife and your job?
—After three years your job still sucks.

Anon

I'm not really a cab driver. I'm just waiting for something better to come along. You know, like death.

Alex Rieger, *Taxi*

—Do you have a job?
—I'm an accountant.
—Chartered?
—Turf.

Penny Warrender and Vince Pinner, *Just Good Friends*

I was a house painter for five years. Five years. I didn't think I'd ever finish that damn house.

John Fox

I was a shepherd once, but I got fired because I always fell asleep during inventory.

John Mendoza

I used to have a job in the Kotex factory. I thought I was making mattresses for mice.

Ray Scott

Ninety-nine point nine per cent of the work of a professional bodyguard consisted of one activity: frowning.

Martin Amis, *Yellow Dog*

Vocation: any badly-paid job which someone has taken out of choice.

Mike Barfield, *Dictionary for our Time*

Never buy anything with a handle on it. It means work.

H. Allen Smith

I went for a job at one of the airlines. The interviewer asked me why I wanted to be a stewardess, and I told her it would be a great chance to meet men... She looked at me and said: 'But you can meet men anywhere.' I said, 'Strapped down?'

Martha Raye

I'm a poor candidate for espionage.

Dolly Parton

A lot of people complain about their dumb boss. What they don't realize is that they'd be out of a job if their dumb boss were any smarter.

Joey Adams

—Griffin! Are you sleeping on the job?
—No. There's a bug in my eye and I'm trying to suffocate him.

Mr Weed and Peter Griffin, *Family Guy*

My husband always felt that marriage and a career don't mix. That is why he's never worked.

Phyllis Diller

My toughest job was being married to Barbra Streisand.

Elliott Gould

My theory is that the hardest work anyone ever does in life is to appear normal.

Edtv

IDLENESS

Laziness: the habit of resting before fatigue sets in.

Jules Renard

Believe me, you gotta get up early if you want to get out of bed.

Groucho Marx

I am not an early riser. The self-respect which other men enjoy in rising early I feel due to me for waking up at all.

William Gerhardie

I always like to have the morning well-aired before I get up.

Beau Brummell

He had once asked...what the old boy most liked in the morning. The reply was: 'Lying in bed on a summer morning, with the window open, listening to the church bells, eating buttered toast with cunty fingers.'

Henry Green

No man who is in a hurry is quite civilized.

Will Durant

I have seen slower people than I am – and more deliberate people than I am – and even quieter, and more listless, and lazier people than I am.
But they were dead.

Mark Twain

I like the word 'indolence'. It makes my laziness seem classy.

Bern Williams

Few women and fewer men have enough character to be idle.

E.V. Lucas

I'm kind of lazy. I'm dating a pregnant woman.

Ron Richards

Never put off till tomorrow what you can do today. It may be made illegal by then.

Anon

MISTAKES

Life is a maze in which we take the wrong turning before we have learned to walk.

Cyril Connolly

Doctors bury their mistakes. Lawyers hang them. But journalists put theirs on the front page.

Anon

To err is human, but to really screw things up requires a financial adviser.

Kathy Lette

All men make mistakes, but married men find out about them sooner.

Red Skelton

If I had to live my life again, I'd make all the same mistakes – only sooner.

Tallulah Bankhead

One of the blessings of being a humorist is that all your mistakes pass off as jokes.

Peter McArthur

—Tiny mistake? £75,000 wasted? Give me an example of a big mistake.
—Letting people find out about it.

Jim Hacker and Sir Humphrey Appleby, *Yes, Minister*

If life had a second edition, how I would correct the proofs.

John Clare, poet

Correction: the following typo appeared in our last bulletin: 'Lunch will be gin at 12:15.' Please correct to read: '12 noon.'

California Bar Association Newsletter

SUCCESS & FAILURE

My mother said: 'You won't amount to anything because you procrastinate.' I said: 'Just wait.'

Judy Tenuta

—What would you like to achieve before you die?
—World peace and a diet pill that really works.

Interviewer and Joan Rivers

I like when a woman has ambition. It's like seeing a dog wearing clothes.

Jack Donaghy, *30 Rock*

My goal is to be able to say, 'Fame and fortune just didn't bring me happiness.'

Lotus Weinstock

You've got a goal. I've got a goal. Now all we need is a football team.

Groucho Marx

If women can sleep their way to the top, how come they aren't there?

Ellen Goodman

You can only sleep your way to the middle.

Dawn Steel

I got what I have now through knowing the right time to tell terrible people when to go to hell.

Leslie Caron

You don't have to be nice to people on the way up if you're not planning to come back down.

Dan G. Stone

I'm a self-made man. Who else would help?

Oscar Levant

When eating an elephant, take one bite at a time.

Creighton W. Abrams

Leroy is a self-made man, which shows what happens when you don't follow directions.

Bill Hoest, cartoon caption

I was a pit bull on the pant leg of opportunity. I wouldn't let go.

George W. Bush

That's the way to get on in the world – by grabbing your opportunities. Why, what's Big Ben but a wrist-watch that saw its chance and made good.

P.G. Wodehouse, *The Small Bachelor*

Don't listen to those who say, 'You're taking too big a chance.' Michelangelo would have painted the Sistine floor, and it would surely be rubbed out by today.

Neil Simon

The secret of success is to know something nobody else knows.

Aristotle Onassis

The secrets of success are a good wife and a steady job. My wife told me.

Howard Nemerov

If at first you don't succeed... buy her another beer.

Slogan on T-shirt

If at first you do succeed – try to hide your astonishment.

Harry F. Banks

Success makes life easier. It doesn't make living easier.

Bruce Springsteen

On every summit you are on the brink of an abyss.

Stanislaw J. Lec

I got a sister who's got me beat in every way. She's 5ft 2". Her husband never has a drink until noon. And she's a beautician. I mean how do you compete with that?

Carla Tortelli, *Cheers*

I feel about as useless as a mom's college degree.

Kenneth Parcell, *30 Rock*

I don't have any leadership qualities. In high school I was president of the German Club; nobody would listen to me. If you can't get Germans to follow orders, who will?

Felix Unger, *The Odd Couple*

One evening when we were in Gerry's, which was predominantly a bar for journalists who liked a drink and actors who were out of work, somebody said: 'What is that terrible smell?' And Keith Waterhouse replied: 'Failure.'

Michael Parkinson

Some people are so far behind in a race that they actually believe they're leading.

Corrado 'Junior' Soprano, *The Sopranos*

Every man has one thing he can do better than anyone else – and usually it's reading his own handwriting.

G. Norman Collie

The penalty of success is to be bored by the attentions of people who formerly snubbed you.

Mary W. Little

BUSINESS

Business is the combination of war and sport.

André Maurois

An executive is an ulcer with authority.

Fred Allen

A 10,000-aspirin job.

Japanese term for executive responsibility

An entrepreneur…is a born schemer and thinker up of things.

Sir Alan Sugar

You and I are such similar creatures. We both screw people for money.

Edward Lewis, businessman, to a hooker, *Pretty Woman*

I want to please every woman, every time.

Stuart Rose, CEO of M&S

A swivel chair has ruined more men than chorus girls or liquor.

Fiorello LaGuardia

Willy was a salesman... He's a man way out there in the blue, riding on a smile and a shoeshine.

Charley, *Death of a Salesman*

—How many calls would you make on a prospect before you'd give up?
—Depends on which one of us dies first.

Sales Associate and Harvey Mackay

An appetite for haggling that would put a Turkish carpet salesman to shame.

Des Dearlove, on Richard Branson

Telephone, telegram and tell-a-woman.

Estée Lauder, maxim for promoting new products

What do you do when your competitor is drowning? Get a live hose and stick it in his mouth.

Ray Kroc, founder of McDonald's

I don't like to hire consultants. They're like castrated bulls – all they can do is advise.

Victor Kiam

Consultants are people who borrow your watch to tell you what time it is and then walk off with it.

Robert Townsend

A consultant's client is someone with a very expensive watch who doesn't know what time it is.

Robert J. Lewis

Five Stages of a Corporate Action: 1) Wild enthusiasm;
2) Disillusionment; 3) Search for the guilty; 4) Conviction of the innocent; 5) Promotion of the uninvolved.

Anon

A monopolist is a fellow who manages to get an elbow on each arm of his theatre chair.

Herbert V. Prochnow

Decision: what a man makes when he can't find anybody to serve on a committee.

Fletcher Knebel

A committee is an animal with four back legs.

John Le Carré

A conference is just an admission that you want somebody to join you in your troubles.

Will Rogers

—How did your meeting go?
—Worse than a dentist. Better than a proctologist.

Catherine Willows and Conrad Ecklie, *CSI*

If you want something done, give it to a busy man – and he'll have his secretary do it.

Anon

—You can't do shorthand, I suppose?
—I don't know. I've never tried.

P.G. Wodehouse, *Eggs, Beans and Crumpets*

You can teach 'em how to type, but you can't teach 'em how to grow tits.

Charlie Wilson, Texan Democrat, who staffed his Washington office with beautiful girls know as 'Charlie's Angels'

If I had ever learned to type, I never would have made brigadier general.

Brigadier General Elizabeth P. Hoisington

Fire her. And don't ever make me talk to a woman that old again.

Jack Donaghy, *30 Rock*

I think that maybe in every company today there is always at least one person who is going crazy slowly.

Joseph Heller

HOBBIES
& LEISURE

HOBBIES &
RECREATIONS

—When I touch my tongue to aluminium foil wrapped around a walnut while holding a toaster oven, I feel a peculiar tingling in my toes – what's wrong with me, Doctor?
—You have too much spare time.

Daniel Pirar, cartoon caption

Recently, I began to feel this void in my life...and I said to myself: 'Dave, all you do with your spare time is sit around and drink beer. You need a hobby.' So I got a hobby. I make beer.

Dave Barry

Twelve kids? What other hobbies have you got?

Groucho Marx

—I've joined the Ramblers' Club.
—Walking or talking?

Listener, *Wake Up to Wogan*

I still have two abiding passions. One is my model railway, the other – women. But the age of 89, I find I am getting a little too old for model railways.

Pierre Monteux

Ambrose Flood had a model railway, but none of us ever saw it, for it was under the floorboards of his bedroom. It was a Tube train, and Ambrose, who was literal-minded, believed that it should accordingly be kept underground.

Hugh Leonard

I'm very bad at Sudoku and crossword puzzles, any kind of pen and paper trivia. I started doing a word search once and then I realised it was a Will Self column.

Jo Caulfield

My favourite crossword clue is: '   ' (3,3,3,1,4). The solution is: Has not got a clue.

Val Gilbert, cruciverbalist

There is nothing that disgusts a man like getting beaten at chess by a woman.

Charles Dudley Warner

I see only one move ahead, but it is always the correct one.

José Raúl Capablanca, Cuban World Chess Champion

There is a new version of Trivial Pursuit. It's called 'The Economist's Edition'. There are 100 questions and 3,000 answers.

President Ronald Reagan

I wanna make a jigsaw puzzle that's 40,000 pieces. And when you finish it, it says 'go outside'.

Demetri Martin

Sailing: the fine art of getting wet and becoming ill while slowly going nowhere at great expense.

Henry Beard

Scuba diving is the closest you can come to going through the back of the wardrobe into a more fabulous world.

Norman Tebbit

I bought one of those frogman suits...jumped in the water and went down about 155 feet... All of a sudden I saw a man walking towards me in a sports jacket and grey flannels...I went up to him, took out a pad and wrote on it: 'What are you doing down here walking about in sports jacket and grey flannels?' And he wrote on the pad: 'I'm drowning.'

Tommy Cooper

Nothing spoils fun like finding out it builds character.

Calvin, *Calvin and Hobbes*

FISHING

Give a man a fish, feed him for a day. Teach a man to fish, and he'll want to come along and drink all your beer.

Bob Ward

Fishing is a passion. I often think that when you are fishing, wildlife comes to you, because you are a peculiarity – a quiet human being.

Iain Duncan Smith

All you need to be a fisherman is patience and a worm.

Herb Shriner

Fishing trip: journey undertaken by one or more anglers to a place where no one can remember when the black flies arrived so early, the ice melted so late, or it rained so much.

Henry Beard

There is no use in your walking five miles to fish when you can depend on being just as unsuccessful nearer home.

Mark Twain

Somebody just back of you while you are fishing is as bad as someone looking over your shoulder while you write a letter to your girl.

Ernest Hemingway

Fly fishing is to fishing as ballet is to walking.

Howell Raines

There are two distinct kinds of visits to tackle-shops: the visit to buy tackle, and the visit which may be described as platonic when, being for some reason unable to fish, we look for an excuse to go in and waste a tackle dealer's time.

Arthur Ransome

This fishing tackle manufacturer I knew had all these flashy green and purple lures. I asked, 'Do fish take these?' 'Charlie,' he said, 'I don't sell these lures to *fish*.'

Charles T. Munger

My biggest worry is that my wife (when I'm dead) will sell my fishing gear for what I said I paid for it.

Koos Brandt

GAMBLING

—What has six balls and screws the poor?
—The lottery.

Anon

I know nothing about racing and any money I put on a horse is a sort of insurance policy to prevent it winning.

Frank Richardson

Gambling promises the poor what property performs for the rich – something for nothing.

George Bernard Shaw

Gosh, I just love gambling here in Vegas. Sure, I may lose $100,000, but the drinks are free, so it evens out!

Karen Walker, *Will and Grace*

Never bet odds-on. If you could buy money, they would sell it at the shop down the road.

Barry Hills

It is surely the epitome of pointlessness to gamble within your limits.

Clement Freud

Bookie: a pickpocket who lets you use your own hands.

Henry Morgan

My favourite occupation is gin rummy – but not together.

W.C. Fields

No wife can endure a gambling husband – unless he is a steady winner.

Lord Dewar

My wife made me join a bridge club. I jump off next Tuesday.

Rodney Dangerfield

CONSUMERISM

There must be more to life than having everything.

Maurice Sendak

The only reason a great many American families don't own an elephant is that they have never been offered an elephant for a dollar down and easy weekly payments.

Mad **magazine**

Marie Antoinette should be living in such an age!

Will Self, on the price of a Jane Asher birthday cake

Just before consumers stop doing something, they do it with a vengeance.

Faith Popcorn, *attrib.*

A lady once offered me a mat, but as I had no room to spare within the house, nor time to spare within or without to shake it, I declined it, preferring to wipe my feet on the sod before my door. It is best to avoid the beginnings of evil.

Henry David Thoreau

If I can't have too many truffles, I'll do without truffles.

Colette

The cost of a thing is the amount of what I call life which is required to be exchanged for it, immediately or in the long run.

Henry David Thoreau

I have the simplest tastes. I am always satisfied with the best.

Oscar Wilde

SHOPPING

—Where does a one-armed man shop?
—At a second-hand store.

Anon

One must choose, in life, between making money and spending it.
There's no time to do both.

Edouard Bourdet

In their hearts women think that it is men's business to earn money
and theirs to spend it.

Arthur Schopenhauer

My wife will buy anything marked down. She brought home two
dresses and an escalator.

Henny Youngman

When it comes to plastic surgery and sushi, never be attracted by
a bargain.

Graham Norton

I love to freak out shop assistants. They ask what size I need, and I
say, 'Extra medium.'

Steven Wright

We're all going into the fitting room to have a fit.

Wanda, *Rose Marie*

I was shopping at IKEA and I decided to grab a ham sandwich
from the kiosk. They gave me two slices of bread, a chunk of ham,
an Allen key and told me to construct it myself. It was nice. The
key was gritty but went down okay.

Darren Casey

There is only one thing for a man to do who is married to a
woman who enjoys spending money, and that is to enjoy earning it.

Ed Howe

HOLIDAY

We hit the sunny beaches where we occupy ourselves keeping the
sun off our skin, the saltwater off our bodies, and the sand out of
our belongings.

Erma Bombeck

Vacation: two weeks on the sunny sands, the rest of the year on the financial rocks.

Sam Ewing

A friend of mine said, 'You want to go to Margate, it's good for rheumatism.' So I did and I got it.

Tommy Cooper

A vacation is having nothing to do and all day to do it in.

Robert Orben

The alternative to a vacation is to stay home and tip every third person you see.

Anon

I've found out what I don't like about family holidays: family.

Anon

A lot of parents pack up their troubles and send them off to a summer camp.

Raymond Duncan

A Jew on a vacation is just looking for a place to sit. A Jew sees a chair, it's a successful vacation.

Jackie Mason

Sunburn is very becoming – but only when it is even – one must be careful not to look like a mixed grill.

Noël Coward

A bikini is not a bikini unless it can be pulled through a wedding ring.

Louis Reard

Speedo? Speedon't!

Dr John Becker, *Becker*

When I go to a nude beach, I always take a ruler, just in case I have to prove something.

Rodney Dangerfield

With me a change of trouble is as good as a vacation.

David Lloyd George

Nudists are like people who do amateur dramatics: those who are most enthusiastic are those who should do it least.

Jeremy Hardy, *The News Quiz*

—Who's the most popular guy at the nudist camp?
—The one who can carry two cups of coffee and a dozen doughnuts at the same time.

Anon

HOTEL

—How do you know you're in a bad hotel?
—When you call reception and say, 'I've got a leak in my sink,' and they say, 'Go ahead.'

Anon

It used to be a good hotel, but that proves nothing – I used to be a good boy.

Mark Twain

My room's so small I put my key in the lock last night and broke a window.

David Feherty

Room service? Send up a larger room!

Groucho Marx

I'm staying in a strange hotel. I called room service for a sandwich and they sent up two hookers.

Bill Maher

When I came into my hotel room last night I found a strange blonde in my bed. I would stand for none of that nonsense! I gave her exactly 24 hours to get out.

Groucho Marx

Why do they put the Gideon Bibles only in the bedrooms, where it's usually too late?

Christopher Morley

A vicar books into a hotel and says to the hotel clerk: 'I hope the porn channel in my room is disabled?' She says: 'No sir, it's just regular porn. You sick bastard.'

Popbitch.com

Those bellhops in Miami are tip-happy. I ordered a deck of playing cards and the bellboy made fifty-two trips to my room.

Henny Youngman

POLITICS

POWER

I was allowed to ring the school-bell for five minutes until everyone was in assembly. It was the beginning of power.

Jeffrey Archer

The wrong sort of people are always in power because they would not be in power if they were not the wrong sort of people.

Jon Wynne-Tyson

Power corrupts; absolute power is really neat!

Donald Regan, President Reagan's Chief of Staff

Lyndon B. Johnson's instinct for power is as primordial as a salmon's going upstream to spawn.

Theodore H. White

The thing women have yet to learn is nobody gives you power. You just take it.

Roseanne

Many a man that could rule a hundred million strangers with an iron hand is careful to take off his shoes in the front hallway when he comes home late at night.

Finlay Peter Dunne

She Tarzan, he Jane.

Andrew Morton, on the relationship
between Victoria and David Beckham

There is no greater human power on earth than the tremendous indignation of the people.

Daniel Webster

Power is the ultimate aphrodisiac.

Henry Kissinger

Power is like a woman you want to stay in bed with forever.

Patrick Anderson

GOVERNMENT

Government is nothing but who collects the money and how do they spend it.

Gore Vidal

In general, the art of government consists in taking as much money as possible from one party of the citizens to give to the other.

Voltaire

—Is it possible that Caesar, the conqueror of the world, has time to occupy himself with such a trifle as our taxes?
—My friend: taxes are the chief business of a conqueror of the world.

Pothinus and Caesar, *Caesar and Cleopatra*

Government's view of the economy could be summed up in a few short phrases: If it moves, tax it. If it keeps moving, regulate it. And if it stops moving, subsidise it.

Ronald Reagan

A welfare state is one that assumes responsibility for the health, happiness and general well-being of all its citizens except the tax-payer.

Boyle's Observation

Governments last as long as the under-taxed can defend themselves against the over-taxed.

Bernard Berenson

A little government and a little luck are necessary in life, but only a fool trusts either of them.

P.J. O'Rourke

ELECTION

Do you ever get the feeling that the only reason we have elections is to find out if the polls were right?

Robert Orben

General or local election: rare opportunity for parents to learn the location of their children's school.

Mike Barfield, *Dictionary for our Time*

In elections, the undecided vote is usually the deciding factor.

Evan Esar

Come canvassing with me and you'll find more cold shoulders than in all the fridges of Smithfield.

Michael Gove, MP

—I can't stop to talk, I just lost my dog!
—Can I help look for it?
—No, it just died.

Elderly Lady and David Cameron, campaigning in Witney, 2001

I did enjoy campaigning, up to a point. Some things I never learned to like. I didn't like to kiss babies, though I didn't mind kissing their mothers.

Pierre Trudeau

Michael Heseltine has been canvassing like a child molester hanging around the lavatories and waiting to pounce on people.

Norman Lamont

Receiving support from Ted Heath is like being measured by an undertaker.

George Gardiner, when the prime minister went to speak for him during a by-election

Don't do anything that indicates that you know you're going to lose. My wife actually wanted to put our house in the constituency up for sale *during* the election campaign. I said that will actually be a little bit revealing.

Gyles Brandreth, before losing his seat as MP for Chester

Things on the whole are much faster in America; people don't *stand for election*, they *run for office*.

Jessica Mitford

The race is as hot and tight as a too-small bathing suit on a too-long car ride back from the beach.

Dan Rather, broadcaster, on US election night, 1996

George McGovern couldn't carry the South if Rhett Butler were his running mate.

Spiro Agnew

We'd all like to vote for the best man, but he's never a candidate.

Kin Hubbard

Vote for the man who promises least; he'll be the least disappointing.

Bernard Baruch

Voters will always go for Santa not Scrooge.

Rachel Sylvester

When I was in the third grade, there was a kid running for office. His slogan was: 'Vote for me and I'll show you my wee-wee.' He won by a landslide.

Dorothy Zbornak, *The Golden Girls*

POLITICIANS

Harold Wilson: all facts, no bloody ideas.

Aneurin Bevan

Better George Brown drunk than Harold Wilson sober.

The Times

John Gummer looks like a tax clerk. By which I suppose I mean he looks somehow like a paper clip, a bit like a going out tray loosely jammed into a coming in tray, a bit like a cold cup of instant coffee at 10.20, a bit like a neon light in a windowless office etc., etc...

Ted Hughes

Clement Attlee brings to the fierce struggle of politics the tepid enthusiasm of a lazy summer afternoon at a cricket match.

Aneurin Bevan

Neville Chamberlain – a good Lord Mayor of Birmingham in a lean year.

Lloyd George

Benjamin Disraeli – a flamingo in a farmyard.

Desmond McCarthy

There is nobody in politics I can remember and no case I can think of in history where a man combined such a powerful political personality with so little intelligence.

Roy Jenkins, on James Callaghan

A second-class intellect but a first-class temperament.

Oliver Wendell Holmes, on President Theodore Roosevelt, *attrib*.

Stephen Byers is the talking equivalent of invisible ink. Within seconds of his speaking you cannot recall a word he has said: he simply wipes himself from your consciousness.

Matthew Parris

R.A. Butler would have been marvellous in medieval politics, creeping about the Vatican; a tremendous intriguer, he always had some marvellous plan...and he loved the press.

Harold Macmillan

Peter Mandelson is a pussycat. By which I mean he is a sleek and mean carnivore who should never be rubbed up the wrong way.

Martin Rowson

Half the time Peter Mandelson was like one of those people who shout at strangers on buses; the other half he resembled a slightly creepy uncle reading a bedtime story.

Simon Hoggart, listening to a speech by Peter Mandelson

If either of them had anything to say, it would matter less that neither has the gift of language. If either had the gift of language, it would matter less that neither has anything to say.

Matthew Parris, listening to a debate between John Major and Neil Kinnock

John Major always came across as the sort of man your granny would knit a cardigan for. Honest John. Nice John. A good man, sadly fallen among Eurosceptics.

Caroline Daniel

If John Major was drowning, his whole life would pass in front of him, and he wouldn't be in it.

Dave Allen

John Major put the 'er' back into Conservative, David Cameron's put the 'con' into Conservative, and Norman Lamont put the VAT into Conservative.

David Miliband

Woody Allen without the jokes.

Simon Hoggart, on Sir Keith Joseph

Jeffrey has a gift for inaccurate precis.

Mary Archer, on her husband

The best way to think about Jeffrey Archer is to treat him as if he comes from another planet. He will drive over a cliff and then be amazed that he's falling. He thinks he's Peter Pan, and he'll never die.

Sheridan Morley

John Prescott – for years we had a deputy prime minister who looked liked a National Express coach-driver.

Rory Bremner

Everything John Prescott touches turns to sewage.

Simon Carr

Tony Benn has had more conversions on the road to Damascus than a Syrian long-distance lorry driver.

Jimmy Reid

David Steel's passed from rising hope to elder statesman without any intervening period whatsoever.

Michael Foot

Margaret Thatcher is the Sybil Fawlty of British Conservatism.

P.D. Morris-Morgan

Margaret Thatcher has no imagination and that means no compassion.

Michael Foot

I would suggest as a memorial to Mrs Thatcher that instead of the usual headstone or statue, a dance floor should be erected over her grave.

Ann Graham

Tony Blair has pushed moderation to extremes.

Robert Maclennan

Describing Tony Blair as Middle East peace envoy is like asking a mosquito to find a cure for malaria.

Rory Bremner

Tony Blair looks like a multi-millionaire playboy, a George Hamilton. That's what happens to Bambi when he gets old.

Lord Tim Bell, 2010

Gordon Brown has, ridiculously, been compared to Stalin. He is no Stalin. He lacks the grip of a leader.

William Rees-Mogg

Gordon Brown...would have been a great statesman in the 19th century, but in this televisual age, with his glowering demeanour, his blind eye and his introversion, he is out of time.

A.C. Grayling

He doesn't do limelight.

Ed Boyle, on Gordon Brown

Like a ticket inspector recently retrained in the art of customer relations, Gordon Brown was all smiles and small talk.

Matthew Parris

Where did Gordon Brown learn to smile? Watching *The Shining*?

Frankie Boyle, *My Shit Life So Far*

Gordon Brown sounds like a Dalek with about three stock phrases... Remember, Daleks always want world domination but they always lose.

Peter Bazalgette

David Miliband always has one expression on his face – it's a mixture of puzzlement and aggression. Which makes me think that he lives in a cul-de-sac. You know when you walk down a cul-de-sac by mistake and you see someone and they sort of look at you like, 'You don't live in a cul-de-sac…'

Frankie Boyle, *Mock the Week*

Boris Johnson's personality is like a hunt ball held in a cricket pavilion.

Clive James

The utensil that scraped Ken Livingstone from the soles of Londoners.

Boris Johnson, Mayor of London, describing himself

The blondest suicide note in history.

Ming Campbell, on Boris Johnson

If you said to most people on the Tube, 'Iain Duncan Smith?' they'd probably say, 'Oh, it's the next stop but one.'

Antony Jay

Iain Duncan Smith: two surnames in search of a hyphen.

Keith Waterhouse

John Redwood is not in fact a human being at all, but a Vulcan, recently landed from the planet of the same name, where merciless logic rules.

Matthew Parris

Theresa May: Lynda Bellingham's serious sister.

The Guardian

A politician with the persona of a sanctimonious Leeds undertaker on a day trip to Bridlington.

Roy Hattersley, on Vince Cable

David Cameron is a bum-faced southern ponce with a tiny washer for a mouth.

Armando Iannucci, *The Audacity of Hype*

The baby face doesn't worry me. It's the baby mind that does.

John Prescott, on David Cameron

It is easy to build a Cameron lookalike. Just simulate the smuggest estate agent you can think of. Or some interchangeable braying twit in a rugby shirt, ruining a local pub just by being there.

Charlie Brooker

If David Cameron hadn't gone to Eton, he'd be managing a Pizza Hut.

Frankie Boyle

Prime Minister, do you now regret, when once asked what your favourite joke was, you replied: 'Nick Clegg.'

Andy Bell, journalist, to David Cameron, after the 2010 election

I met Nick Clegg the other day, and he said, 'Can you do me?' I said, 'No, can you?'

Rory Bremner, impressionist

HOUSE OF LORDS

If you think there are some rum folk in the Commons, wait until you see who fetches up in a directly elected Lords.

George Walden

I may be here because my forefather got pissed with Pitt, but that's better than those newcomers who are just Blair's tennis partners.

Earl of Onslow, on the composition of the House of Lords, 2003

Obviously you do get one or two people in the Lords who are a bit odd, but you get nutters everywhere.

Baroness Strange

Ministers moving to the House of Lords receive approbation, elevation and castration, all in one stroke.

Sir Humphrey Appleby, *Yes, Minister*

The other night I dreamed that I was addressing the House of Lords. Then I woke up and, by God, I was!

Duke of Devonshire

I will be sad, if I look up or down after my death and don't see my son asleep on the same benches on which I slept.

Lord Onslow, opposing reforms

When I'm sitting on the Woolsack in the House of Lords I amuse myself by saying 'Bollocks' *sotto voce* to the bishops.

Lord Hailsham

The reason the bishops' benches in the House of Lords are the only ones in the chamber which have arms to them is to stop drunken bishops rolling off the seats and onto the floor, thus causing a scandal.

Jo Grimond, MP

POLITICAL SPEECHES

Speechwriting is to writing as Muzak is to music.

Aram Bakshian, political speechwriter

When Nelson Rockefeller buys a Picasso, he doesn't hire four housepainters to improve it.

Henry Kissinger, to Hugh Morrow, who had asked Rockefeller's speechwriting staff to edit Kissinger's draft of a speech

A good political speech is not one in which you can prove that the man is telling the truth; it is one where no one else can prove he is lying.

Sir Humphrey Appleby, *Yes, Minister*

All great soundbites happen by accident...as part of the natural expression of the text. They are part of the tapestry, they aren't a little flower somebody sewed on.

Peggy Noonan

It just shows, what any member of Parliament will tell you, that if you want real oratory, the preliminary noggin is essential. Unless pie-eyed, you cannot hope to grip.

P.G. Wodehouse, *Right Ho, Jeeves*

I noticed first the verb-free sentences, which Tony Blair still uses today: 'Our people, prosperous and secure. Our children, meeting the challenge...' He might use up to 200 in one speech, making it sound like oratorical Muzak, conveying little but a sense of wellbeing.

Simon Hoggart

William Hague makes rather good speeches. They've got verbs in them.

Douglas Hurd

I stand up when he nudges me. I sit down when they pull my coat.

Ernest Bevin

FOREIGN AFFAIRS & DIPLOMACY

Vladimir Putin doesn't have a foreign policy. He has a price.

Orlando Figes

Having a friend doesn't mean you are kneeling in front of him.

Gilles Duceppe, on the relationship between Canada and the USA, *attrib*.

No nation has friends – only interests.

Charles de Gaulle

Two nations which have never fought each other can never be real friends.

Miles Kington

There is only one thing worse than fighting with allies, and that is fighting without them.

Winston Churchill

Alliance: in international politics, the union of two thieves who have their hands so deeply inserted in each other's pockets that they cannot separately plunder a third.

Ambrose Bierce

Gratitude, like love, is never a dependable international emotion.

Joseph Alsop

Love for the same thing never makes allies. It's always hate for the same thing.

Howard Spring

Treaties are like roses and young girls. They last while they last.

Charles de Gaulle

The United Nations is the accepted forum for the expression of international hatred.

Sir Humphrey Appleby, *Yes, Prime Minister*

Ultimatum: in diplomacy, a last demand before resorting to concessions.

Ambrose Bierce

Diplomat: a man who thinks twice before saying nothing.

Frederick Sawyer

There is nothing more likely to start disagreement among people or countries than an agreement.

E.B. White

Forever poised between a cliché and an indiscretion.

Harold Macmillan, on the life of a Foreign Secretary

BUREAUCRACY

—How many bureaucrats does it take to change a light bulb?
—Two. One to assure us that everything possible is being done while the other screws the bulb into a hot water tap.

***Voice for Health* magazine**

I came to Number 11 reluctantly, I can tell you, but after I'd lined up all the former staff and shot them I felt a good deal better. 'Start as you mean to go on,' has always been good advice.

**Newly appointed Chancellor of the Exchequer,
in a satirical article written for *Punch* magazine by Alan Hackney**

Poor fellow, he suffers from files.

Aneurin Bevan, on administrator, Sir Walter Citrine

This place needs a laxative.

Bob Geldof, on red tape at the European Parliament, Strasbourg

The Pentagon is like a log going down the river with 25,000 ants on it, each thinking he's steering the log.

Henry S. Rowen

The Pentagon was so huge people were said to spend days and even weeks wandering its endless corridors trying to find their way out. One woman was said to have told a guard she was in labour and needed help in getting to a maternity hospital. He said: 'Madam, you should not have come in here in that condition.' 'When I came in here,' she answered, 'I wasn't.'

David Brinkley

Asking a town hall to slim down its staff is like asking an alcoholic to blow up a distillery.

Sir Humphrey Appleby, *Yes, Minister*

I confidently expect that we shall continue to be grouped with mothers-in-law and Wigan Pier as one of the recognized objects of ridicule.

Edward Bridges, on civil servants

The only thing that saves us from bureaucracy is its inefficiency.

Eugene McCarthy

The British created a civil service job in 1803 calling for a man to stand on the Cliffs of Dover with a spyglass. He was supposed to ring a bell if he saw Napoleon coming. The job was abolished in 1945.

Robert Sobel

ARTS & ENTERTAINMENT

MUSIC

—How do you make a bandstand?
—Take away their chairs.

Anon

A music lover is one who when told that Pamela Anderson sings in the bath, puts his ear to the keyhole.

Anon

Whatever music sounds like, I am glad to say that it does not sound in the smallest degree like German.

Oscar Wilde

Music is the only language in which you cannot say a mean or sarcastic thing.

John Erskine

Making music is like making love: the act is always the same, but each time it's different.

Arthur Rubinstein

Some people can carry a tune, but they seem to stagger under the load.

Richard Armour

—You sing like the Spice Girls.
—Thanks.
—Unfortunately, it wasn't a compliment.

Simon Cowell and Contestant, *Pop Idol*

When you listen to Mozart, the silence that follows is still Mozart.

Sacha Guitry

Did anyone ever tell you, you have the voice of a songbird...slowly dying in tar?

Captain Benjamin 'Hawkeye' Pierce, *M*A*S*H*

The first Sunday I sang in the church choir, 200 people changed their religion.

Fred Allen

Y'know, I could sing like Caruso if I wanted to...but he's already done it.

Tom Waits

Once men sang together round a table in chorus; now one man sings alone for the absurd reason that he can sing better. If scientific civilization goes on...only one man will laugh, because he can laugh better than the rest.

G.K. Chesterton

A young composer had written two pieces of music and asked the great Rossini to hear them both and say which he preferred. He duly played one piece, whereupon Rossini intervened. 'You need not play any more,' he said, 'I prefer the other one.'

Kenneth Edwards

The next piece I composed was written in three flats – I moved three times while writing it.

Victor Borge

Had Wagner been a little more human, he would have been truly divine.

Claude Debussy

Chopin's music is excellent on rainy afternoons in winter, with the fire burning, the shaker full, and the girl somewhat silly.

H.L. Mencken

Brahms feels with his head and thinks with his heart.

Louis Ehlert

Of Schubert I hesitate to speak... His merest belch was as lovely as the song of the sirens. He sweated beauty as naturally as a Christian sweats hate.

H.L. Mencken

If wind and water could write music it would sound like Benjamin Britten's.

Yehudi Menuhin

I am sure my music has a taste of codfish in it.

Edvard Grieg

One has in one's mouth the bizarre and charming taste of a pink sweet stuffed with snow.

Claude Debussy, on Edvard Grieg

Elgar – great gusts of roast-beef music...

Laurie Lee

My music is best understood by children and animals.

Igor Stravinsky

For Strauss, the composer, I take my hat off; for Strauss the man I put it on again.

Arturo Toscanini, on Johann Strauss Jr., the 'Waltz King'

I prefer the company of bankers to musicians, because musicians only want to talk about money.

Jean Sibelius, Finnish composer

Bach on the wrong notes.

Sergei Prokofiev, on Igor Stravinsky

At first I thought I should be a second Beethoven; presently I found that to be another Schubert would be good; then, gradually...I was resigned to be a Humperdinck.

Engelbert Humperdinck, composer

If the best thing a composer can be is dead, the next best thing he can be is German. One of the worst things he can possibly be, still, is American.

Milton Babbitt

I thought being a Beatle would be a great way to get out of Birmingham. I used to dream that Paul McCartney would marry my sister. That was going to be my ticket into the Beatles. Unfortunately, Paul wouldn't have liked my sister.

Ozzy Osbourne

John Cage was refreshing but not very bright. His freshness came from an absence of knowledge.

Pierre Boulez

There is no female Mozart because there is no female Jack the Ripper.

Camille Paglia

'Great' conductors, like 'great' actors, soon become unable to play anything but themselves.

Igor Stravinsky

The conductor has the advantage of not seeing the audience.

André Kostelanetz

I don't hire women for my orchestra because if they're pretty, they distract my musicians, and if they're not, they distract me.

Thomas Beecham

Listening to music on records is like being kissed over the telephone.

George Szell, conductor, and champion of live music

Having verse set to music is like looking at a painting through a stained glass window.

Paul Valéry, poet

If the music doesn't say it, how can the words say it for the music?

John Coltrane

Words make you think thoughts. Music makes you feel a feeling. But a song makes you feel a thought.

E.Y. Harburg

In writing songs I've learned as much from Cézanne as I have from Woody Guthrie.

Bob Dylan

The English language is a difficult tool to work with. Two of the hardest words in the language to rhyme are 'life' and 'love'. Of all words! In Italian, easy. But not English.

Stephen Sondheim, on writing lyrics

I was very proud to work with the great George Gershwin, and I would have done it for nothing, which I did.

Howard Dietz, lyricist

Ninety-nine per cent of the world's lovers are not with their first choice. That's what makes the jukebox play.

Willie Nelson

The test of a good song is, can you sing it around a campfire, or, could you imagine Elvis singing it?

Mark Ronson, music producer

Wings – they're the band the Beatles could have been.

Alan Partridge

Even John Peel used to pop by to see how I was getting on, pre-Womble, never post-Womble.

Mike Batt

Disco is from hell, okay? And not the cool part with all the murderers, but the lame-ass part where all the bad accountants live.

Steven Hyde, *That 70s Show*

Italians tend to break down into two kinds of people: Lucky Luciano or Michelangelo. Frank Sinatra's an exception. He's both.

Gene DiNovo

Frank Sinatra is a singer who comes along once in a lifetime, but why did he have to come in my lifetime?

Bing Crosby

To Sinatra, a microphone is as real as a girl waiting to be kissed.

E.B. White

I could go on stage and make a pizza and they'd still come to see me.

Frank Sinatra

Amy Winehouse is more famous for her drinking and drug-taking than her singing. If only the same were true of Céline Dion.

Sandi Toksvig, *The News Quiz*

Michael Jackson will be remembered for how he touched people.

Martine McCutcheon

Paul Weller is like Victor Meldrew with a suntan.

Noel Gallagher

They're usually very sweet underneath. But they look like some sort of wet dream of Himmler's.

Stephen Fry, on Emos and Goths

Glastonbury was very wet and muddy. There was trench foot, dysentery, peaches...all the Geldof daughters.

Sean Lock, *8 Out of 10 Cats*

Thank God the Spice Girls reunion is over. The only way I want to see Geri Halliwell draped in a Union Flag again is if she died in battle.

Frankie Boyle

—You haven't mentioned Elvis Presley.
—I seldom do unless I stub my toe.

Interviewer and Groucho Marx

Your last album sold 2.5 million copies. How come I don't know anybody who owns one?

Craig Kilborn, to guest, Joey Lawrence

It's like an act of murder: you play with intent to commit something.

Duke Ellington, on jazz

I think I had it in the back of my mind that I wanted to sound like a dry Martini.

Paul Desmond, saxophonist

You can taste a word.

Pearl Bailey, singer

—Your band must arrive on the film-set promptly at 8 o'clock in the morning.
—Jesus Christ, my boys don't even start vomiting till eleven.

Producer and Tommy Dorsey

I never really liked jazz. It always sounded to me like scribble.

Jac Naylor, *Holby City*

It's like living in a house where everything's painted red.
Paul Desmond, listening to the 'free jazz' of Ornette Coleman

Play us a medley of your hit.
Oscar Levant, to George Gershwin

Cabaret singer, Blossom Dearie...offers a tiny sound that without a microphone would not reach the second floor of a doll's house.
Whitney Balliett

I never knew how good our songs were until I heard Ella Fitzgerald sing them.
Ira Gershwin

Ella Fitzgerald had a vocal range so wide you needed an elevator to go from the top to the bottom.
Music Journalist

Ella Fitzgerald could sing the California telephone directory with a broken jaw and make it sound good.
Jazz Fan

'Did I Shave My Legs For This?'
Country music song title, Deana Carter & Rhonda Hart

You don't understand country and western music. It's about the real things in life – murder, train wrecks, amputations, faucets leakin' in the night...
Charlie Haggars, *Mary Hartman, Mary Hartman*

Play a country and western song backwards and what happens? You get your wife back, your dog back and you sober up.
James Woods

I had to get rich so I could afford to sing like I was poor again.
Dolly Parton

'If the Phone Doesn't Ring, It's Me'
Country music song title, Jimmy Buffett, Waylon Jennings & Michael Utley

OPERA

And for my next trick I'm going to make my boyfriend disappear. I say the magic word: Opera!

Caroline Duffy, *Caroline in the City*

Opera is a form of entertainment where there is always too much singing.

Claude Debussy

To the opera one goes either for want of any other interest or to facilitate digestion.

Voltaire

Harrods' Food Hall had yielded up its dead.

Jonathan Miller, on Royal Opera House audiences

Opera in English is, in the main, just about as sensible as baseball in Italian.

H.L. Mencken

Sleep is an excellent way of listening to opera.

James Stephens

Every theatre is a madhouse, but an opera theatre is the ward for the incurables.

Franz Schalk, conductor

The tenor voice differs as much from all other human voices as the French horn differs from a piccolo. It has more wolf tones.

H.L. Mencken

Pavarotti's vocal cords were kissed by God.

Harold Schoenberg

—Are you a slave to your voice?
—Yes, but a slave in a golden cage.

Reporter and Luciano Pavarotti

My voice is not so much *bel canto* as *can belto*.

Harry Secombe

One cracked top note will ruin the whole evening... It is exactly like a bullfight. You are not allowed one mistake.

Luciano Pavarotti

Pavarotti's greatest achievement: bringing football to the middle classes.

Gerry Bond

One fart from Caruso would drown out all the tenors on stage today.

Titta Ruffo

Regard your voice as capital in the bank. When you go to sing, do not draw on your bank account. Sing on your interest and your voice will last.

Lauritz Melchior

If you think you've hit a false note, sing loud. When in doubt, sing loud.

Robert Merrill

A healthy sex life. Best thing in the world for a woman's voice.

Leontyne Price, soprano

The soprano sounded like the brakes on the Rome Express.

Charles Winthrop, *Serenade*

She was a singer who had to take any note above 'A' with her eyebrows.

Montague Glass

Her singing was mutiny on the high Cs.

Hedda Hopper

I don't like raised voices; they suggest domestic discord.

Laurie Lee, on his dislike of operatic voices

Stopera!

Graffiti outside a proposed opera house in Holland

DANCE

—Why do Morris Dancers wear bells?
—So they can annoy blind people as well.

Anon

I went to my little niece's tap-dance recital the other day after a few too many beers and I got thrown out cos apparently you're not supposed to stuff the dollar-bills into the leotards.

Tom Cotter

Dancing makes me look like a coma victim being stood up and zapped with a cattle prod.

Mark Corrigan, *Peep Show*

A good education is usually harmful to a dancer. A good calf is better than a good head.

Agnes de Mille, choreographer

There's half a millimetre of Lycra between dancing and sex.

Otto Bathurst

Cynthia was a burlesque queen. I used to love the cute way she'd throw her leg up in the air. Then catch it coming down!

Milton Berle

Fred Astaire was as born to the dance as some men are born to the priesthood.

Tom Shales

Watching the nondancing, nonsinging Astaire is like watching a grounded skylark.

Vincent Canby, on Fred Astaire

Ballroom dancing is the most marvellous business to be in because all the girls are beautiful and all the blokes are gay.

Len Goodman, judge, *Strictly Come Dancing*

Remember those magical nights, Cynthia? We'd dance cheek to cheek. I'd rub my stubble against yours.

Milton Berle

Poofs' football.

John Osborne, on ballet

I'm a guy who likes to keep score. With ballet I can't tell who's ahead.

Fiorella La Guardia

Even the ears must dance!

Natalia Makarova

There are some things it is foolish to try to indicate in a ballet: you cannot indicate your mother-in-law and be readily understood.

George Balanchine

ART

Art is a misquotation of something already heard. Thus, it becomes a quotation of something never heard.

Ned Rorem

I don't know what art is. If it's on the wall at Sotheby's by definition it is art.

Damien Hirst

Art is always the replacement of indifference by attention.

Guy Davenport

I can never pass by the Metropolitan Museum of Art in New York without thinking of it not as a gallery of living portraits but as a cemetery of tax-deductible wealth.

Lewis H. Lapham

All you learn from the art museum is how to keep your mouth shut and how to walk without making squeaky sounds with your shoes.

Curly Sue, *Curly Sue*

Impressionist paintings' prices have become so exorbitant that I can now only afford the frames.

Jeffrey Archer

John Constable observed a landscape so intently and quietly that, while he sat, a field-mouse entered his coat-pocket and fell asleep there.

C.R. Leslie

I have long held the view that Van Gogh's 'Letters to Theo' is a far greater work of art than all his canvases put together.

Henry Miller

You want to know how to paint a perfect painting? It's easy. Make yourself perfect, and then just paint naturally.

Robert Pirsig

Three things that are never drawn or painted the way they really look: a Christmas tree, a star in the sky, and a very rich but ugly person.

Miles Kington

The windmill was invented for the sole purpose of filling up the blank bits in the back of 16th-century Flemish paintings.

Alan Coren

Flesh was the reason why oil painting was invented.

Willem de Kooning

Nudity is to art what a ball is to football.

Antony Gormley

What is the difference between art and pornography?
A government grant.

Peter Griffin, *Family Guy*

If you pay enough for pornography it becomes art.

Caller, *Stephen Nolan Show*, Radio 5 Live

Picasso had his blue period. And I'm in my blonde period.

Hugh Hefner

I have a predilection for painting that lends joyousness to a wall.

Pierre-Auguste Renoir

Part of what painting is, is something to look great over the sofa.

Damien Hirst

At one point I found myself standing before an oil of a horse that I figured was probably a self-portrait judging from the general execution.

Peter De Vries

It was touching to see Alma Tadema's delight at finding (in the Grafton Gallery) pictures demonstrably worse than his own.

Edward Marsh

An age is best revealed by its artists of the second rank.

Geoffrey Wolff

One of my dogs jumped through an Augustus John when I worked at Christie's. When we repaired it, it was marginally better than before.

Brian Sewell, art critic

Henri de Toulouse-Lautrec's paintings were almost entirely painted in absinthe.

Gustav Moreau

Let's go and get drunk on light again – it has the power to console.

Georges Seurat

Matisse was accused of doing things any child could do, and he answered very cheerfully, 'Yes, but not what *you* could do.'

Allan Kaprow

Isn't art which needs explaining as pointless as jokes which do?

Paul Whittle

Picasso was constantly upsetting the verb 'to see'.

Roberto Matta

They ought to put out the eyes of painters as they do goldfinches in order that they can sing better.

Pablo Picasso

What he burned to do, as Velázquez would have burned to do if he had lived today, was to think of another Mickey Mouse and then give up work and watch the money roll in.

P.G. Wodehouse, *Buried Treasure*

Picasso would spit in people's eye but people would frame the spit and sell it.

Roberto Matta

Pop Art is the advertising art advertising itself as art that hates advertising.

Harold Rosenberg

A genius with the IQ of a moron.

Gore Vidal, on Andy Warhol

An artist cannot speak about his art any more than a plant can discuss horticulture.

Jean Cocteau

Damien Hirst... the artist who can transform a pickled bovine into a cash cow.

Rachel Campbell-Johnson

It's always good to remember that people find it easier to name ten artists from any century than ten politicians.

John Heath-Stubbs

SCULPTURE

Sculpture is the stuff you trip over when you are backing up trying to look at a painting.

Jules Olitski

Sculpture is the art of the hole and the lump.

Auguste Rodin

We sculptors are generally less nervy than painters because we get a chance to hammer out our neuroses.

Henry Moore

He didn't like heads, did he?

John Prescott, opening an exhibition of Henry Moore's sculptures

To be a sculptor you need to be one part artist and nine parts navvy.
John Skeaping

For Alberto Giacometti, to sculpt is to take the fat off space.
Jean-Paul Sartre

I saw the angel in the marble and carved until I set him free.
Michelangelo Buonarroti

A great sculpture can roll down a hill without breaking.
Michelangelo Buonarroti

—A Hollywood statistician has found that you have the same dimensions as the Venus de Milo.
—I've got it on her. I've got two arms and I know how to use them. Besides, dearie, I'm not marble.

Reporter and Mae West

Marble and flesh look so different that nude statues need never bring a blush to anyone's cheek.
Francis Turner Palgrave

There cannot be another Michelangelo in today's society because our faith in man is too weak.
André Malraux

PHOTOGRAPHY

Do you think you can manage a smile? It's only for a fiftieth of a second.
Frank Modell

Photography is not art. It's pressing buttons. People take it up because they can't draw.
Lord Snowdon

The photographer is like the cod, which produces a million eggs in order that one may reach maturity.
George Bernard Shaw

Photographing a cake can be art.

Irving Penn

Eugène Atget couldn't have cared less about seeing the sights. Not once, in almost 40 years behind a camera, did he point it at the Eiffel Tower.

Anthony Lane, on the French photographer

FILM & HOLLYWOOD

We go to the movies to be entertained, not to see rape, ransacking, pillage and looting. We can get all that in the stock market.

Kennedy Gammage

A good film is when the price of the admission, the dinner and the babysitter was well worth it.

Alfred Hitchcock

People always ask me, 'Did you see Larry's latest movie?' I always say, 'No, but I flushed a ten dollar bill down the toilet, so I feel like I've seen it.'

Jeff Foxworthy

That movie left the theater so fast they held the premiere at Blockbuster.

Jeffrey Ross

If movie theatres had windows, I would have jumped out of one by the end of *Love Actually*.

Stephanie Zacharek

Don't Look Now was so boring I let my hand wander into the crotch of my companion and the only reaction was the line, 'Any diversion is welcome.'

Kenneth Williams

I've only actually sat through 4 movies in 10 years. There's nothing in my contract that says I have to see the stuff. I clocked in and clocked out.

Robert Mitchum

Hollywood is full of genius. All it lacks is talent.

Henri Bernstein

God felt sorry for actors so he created Hollywood to give them a place in the sun and a swimming pool. The price they had to pay was to surrender their talent.

Cedric Hardwicke

Hollywood is Disneyland staged by Dante. You imagine purgatory is like this, except that the parking is not so good.

Robin Williams

Hollywood is a place where they'll pay you a thousand dollars for a kiss and fifty cents for your soul.

Marilyn Monroe

You can't find true affection in Hollywood because everyone does the fake affection so well.

Carrie Fisher

Hollywood is a town that will nice you to death.

Mel Brooks

If you stay in Beverly Hills too long, you become a Mercedes.

Dustin Hoffman

—Would you do a *Rocky 5*?
—What am I gonna fight? Arthritis?
Jonathan Ross and Sylvester Stallone, *The Jonathan Ross Show*

The Rocky Horror Picture Show: A Sly Stallone retrospective.

Russell Beland

All you need to make a movie is a girl and a gun.

Jean-Luc Godard

I prefer films to newspapers because papers tell lies about real people and films tell the truth about imaginary ones.

G.K. Chesterton

I like movie stills better than the movies. Movies are too long, it bores me after an hour.

Karl Lagerfeld

You are not allowed to be anything but completely polite in Hollywood. It is a comedy of manners. But it is a world of bed-wetters.

Rupert Everett

There are just two stories: going on a journey and a stranger comes to town.

John Gardner

A story should have a beginning, a middle and an end – but not necessarily in that order.

Jean-Luc Godard

Being a writer is like having homework every night for the rest of your life.

Lawrence Kasdan, screenwriter

While in Europe, Eugene O'Neill received a cable on behalf of Jean Harlow, explaining that Miss Harlow wanted the best available American dramatist to write a screenplay for her. Would O'Neill please cable back, collect, confining his answer to 20 words. O'Neill cabled: 'No No No No No No No No No No No No No No No No No No No No O'Neill.'

Croswell Bowen

In this business we make movies. American movies. Leave the films to the French.

Sam Shepard

For some reason, I'm more appreciated in France than I am back home. The subtitles must be incredibly good.

Woody Allen

I don't write pictures about tomatoes that eat people. I write pictures about people who eat tomatoes.

Julius Epstein

It's a bit like leaving your teenage daughter on Jack Nicholson's doorstep; you know no good will come of it.

Unidentified British Author, on selling their novel to Hollywood

Studio heads have foreheads by dint of electrolysis.

S.J. Perelman

Metro-Goldwyn-Merde

Dorothy Parker

People ask me if I went to film school. And I tell them: No, I went to films.

Quentin Tarantino

At work, he is two people – Mr Hyde and Mr Hyde.

Harry Kurnitz, on Billy Wilder

I always thought the real violence in Hollywood isn't what's on the screen. It's what you have to do to raise the money.

David Mamet

Hollywood people don't like making movies. They like making deals.

Roman Polanski

—Movies cost millions of dollars to make.
—That's after gross net deduction profit percentage deferment 10 per cent of the net. Cash, every movie cost $2,184.

Dave and Bobby Bowfinger, *Bowfinger*

THEATRE

The English theatre reminds me of a glorious pool table: great legs, a beautiful green felt top and no balls!

Kenneth Tynan

I am unable to pass a theatre without wanting to walk in, and am unable to listen to a single word from an actor without wanting to walk out again.

Howard Jacobson

One goes to the theatre mainly for the intermissions.

Antoni Slonimski

Long experience has taught me that in England nobody goes to the theatre unless he or she has bronchitis.

James Agate

Sore throat and headache; the responsibility, I'm sure, of the occupant of row A in the royal circle, seat no. 4, on Thursday night.

Alec Guinness, diary entry, 22 Oct. 1995

When you visit a West End theatre…it's like sitting in an Anderson shelter in the Imperial War Museum as part of the Blitz Experience.

Sir Richard Eyre, on the dilapidated state of British theatre buildings

The most famous building in the heart of Dublin is the architecturally undistinguished Abbey Theatre, once the city morgue and now entirely restored to its original purpose.

Frank O'Connor

I had no experience of going to the theatre before I became an actor. When I first got a job at the National, I told my dad and he thought I was working on the horse-race.

Eddie Marsan

I started at the Windmill Theatre in 1949. My father didn't want to me appear there. He said I would see things I shouldn't really see. He was correct. On my third day I saw my father sitting in the front row.

Arthur English

There are two kinds of director in the theatre. Those who think they are God, and those who are certain of it.

Rhetta Hughes

In the theatre, the director is God; unfortunately, the actors are atheists.

Žarko Petan

I was once watching the theatre director, John Dexter, rehearsing a piece, when one of the actors asked him how he should play a particular scene. 'Play it,' advised Dexter silkily, 'as if you could act.'

Keith Waterhouse

Two white-haired ladies, wearing floral dresses, as they left the theatre after seeing Chekhov's *The Cherry Orchard*: 'Well, I thought it was very enjoyable, didn't you, Mary? But why on earth they had to set it in Russia is beyond me.'

Maureen Lipman, *overheard*

—I'm in an off-Broadway production of *The Vagina Monologues*.
We talk a lot about vaginas.
—That's how I spent college.

Calista Flockhart and David Letterman

When Coral Browne attended the first night of a Peter Brook
production, the opening scene revealed a huge phallus about 15
feet high. 'No one we know,' said Coral to her companion.

***Spectator* magazine**

—Wake up you old fool, you slept through the show!
—Who's a fool? *You* watched it.

Stadler and Waldorf, *The Muppet Show*

You have to settle down to Eugene O'Neill like three day cricket:
then the slowness becomes a virtue.

Peter Jenkins

When you leave the theatre, if you don't walk several blocks in the
wrong direction, the performance has been a failure.

Edith Evans

All I hope now is the dog hasn't been sick in the car.

**One Playgoer to another, leaving the Old Vic
after seeing Peter O'Toole in *Macbeth*, *overheard***

FAME & CELEBRITY

Actor David Carradine has been found dead in a wardrobe in his
Bangkok hotel room, after 'accidentally' hanging himself while
attempting auto-erotic asphyxiation. He was best known for his
role as Kwai Chang Caine in the TV series *Kung Fu*. Well, not
anymore he's not.

Frankie Boyle

Fame means millions of people have a wrong idea of who you are.

Erica Jong

One day you are a signature, next day you're an autograph.

Billy Wilder

—Oh, Miss West, I've heard so much about you!
—Yeah, honey, but you can't prove a thing.

Fan and Mae West

I was in a bookshop in Ireland recently and a guy came up to me and said, 'Are you who you think you are?'

Paul Merton

You're never who you think you are. Sometime in the 1980s, an old lady approached me and asked, 'Mr Elton, may I have your autograph?' I told her that I wasn't Elton but David Bowie. She replied, 'Oh, thank goodness. I couldn't stand his red hair and all that make up.'

David Bowie

It's like having Alzheimer's disease. You don't know anybody, but they all know you.

Tony Curtis

What makes a star a star is not that 'indefinable something extra'...
What makes a star a star is that indefinable something MISSING.

Julie Burchill

—Is that a star over there?
—No, that's Ted Danson.

Nancy Lee and Hank Gordon, *Doc Hollywood*

When rulers are ruthless and priests are randy, actors become role models.

Mavor Moore

Carroll Levis, the talent-scout, discovered me. He lifted up a manhole cover and there I was!

Harold Berens

Glamour girl Katie Price did a book signing last week that lasted nearly two hours. To be fair, she didn't take quite so long to sign the second book.

Frank Skinner

I don't sign parts of the body, even if they're still attached.

Terry Pratchett

Writing is my trade and I exercise it only when I am obliged to. It would never be fair to ask a doctor for one of his corpses to remember him by.

Mark Twain, declining a request for an autograph

A celebrity is a person who works hard all his life to become well known, and then wears dark glasses to avoid being recognized.

Fred Allen

Joan Collins is a proper celebrity. She sunbathes in a turban and red lipstick.

Victoria Beckham

The most intolerable people are provincial celebrities.

Anton Chekhov

I made quite a name for myself back home. I left when I found out what it was.

Herb Shriner

They've put a plaque on the wall of the house where I was born. It says: condemned.

Arthur Askey

With fame I become more and more stupid, which of course is a very common phenomenon.

Albert Einstein

My persona don't really work without fame. Without fame, this haircut could be mistaken for mental illness.

Russell Brand

In America I had two secretaries – one for autographs and the other for locks of hair. Within six months one had died of writer's cramp, and the other was completely bald.

Oscar Wilde

Posh and Becks will need more of a talent than just acting like air is absolutely delicious...

Mandy Stadtmiller, after the Beckhams' move to Los Angeles, 2007

Censure is the tax a man pays to the public for being eminent.

Jonathan Swift

If you put a brown jug of water on TV for five minutes a night, it will get fan mail.

Michael Aspel, *attrib.*

Being famous means that you can get a table in a restaurant. But then you've got to go past a line of people who can't get a table, and that's a bad feeling.

Hugh Laurie

The famous are balloons far up in the sky, to be envied for their quiet freedom or shot down as enemies.

Arthur Miller

When I hear a man applauded by the mob I always feel a pang of pity for him. All he has to do to be hissed is to live long enough.

H.L. Mencken

I was on a bus and I heard someone say: 'I saw one of those Two Fat ladies the other day – not the dead one.'

Kevin Ashman

TELEVISION

There are three great moments in a man's life: when he buys a house, a car, and a new TV.

Archie Bunker, *All in the Family*

The human race is divided into two distinct groups: those who walk into rooms and automatically turn television sets on, and those who walk into rooms and automatically turn them off. The trouble is that they end up marrying each other.

Raymond Shaw, *The Manchurian Candidate*

My husband wanted one of those big-screen TVs for his birthday. I just moved his chair closer to the one we already have.

Wendy Liebman

Daddy, tell us again how when you were a boy you had to walk all the way across the room to change channels.

Anon

When I was your age, television was called books.

Grandpa, *The Princess Bride*

When I got my first TV set, I stopped caring so much about having close relationships with other people... I started an affair with my television.

Andy Warhol

Television's far more entertaining and much less trouble than a wife would be.

George Boar

Television: teacher... mother... secret lover!

Homer Simpson

Television is a method to deliver advertising like a cigarette is a method to deliver nicotine.

Bill Maher

Television – a medium, so called because it is neither rare nor well-done.

Ernie Kovacs

COMEDY

There are three golden rules of comedy: 1) If in doubt, wobble about; 2) If that don't work, fall over; 3) If that don't work – knob out!

Malcolm Hardee

My favourite noise in comedy is the laugh followed by the sharp intake of breath.

Jimmy Carr

Bad Taste: the jokes about atrocities rather than those atrocities themselves, oddly.

Mike Barfield, *Dictionary for our Time*

A person reveals his character by nothing so clearly as the joke he resents.

Georg Christoph Lichtenberg

Never forget that the following take themselves seriously: politicians, vegetarians, advanced thinkers and gentlemen in the care of warders and male nurses.

D.B. Wyndham-Lewis

Say I make a 'joke' and it doesn't appeal to you, you are annoyed rather than amused. Annoyed, simply because you haven't found out how to unlaugh.

Flann O'Brien

Gay audiences will laugh at anything except Barbra Streisand. If you dare to say she's cross-eyed... I have one joke in my act that she can cross the street without looking to the right or the left. And they just go 'huh'.

Joan Rivers

What is this, an audience or a jury?

Johnny Carson, after a joke bombed

I don't mind when my jokes die because they go to Heaven and get 72 virgin jokes.

Omar Marzouk

To me, clowns aren't funny. In fact, they're kind of scary. I've wondered where this started, and I think it goes back to the time I went to the circus and a clown killed my dad.

Jack Handey

Humour is falling downstairs if you do it while in the act of warning your wife not to.

Kenneth Bird

Looking over old *Punche*s. Am struck with the frequent wrong direction of satire, and of commendation, when seen by the light of later days.

Thomas Hardy

If you crack a joke in London, people laugh. If you crack a joke in Hollywood, they say, 'You're funny.'

Rhys Ifans

A very little wit is valued in a woman, as we are pleased with a few words spoken plain by a parrot.

Jonathan Swift

Charlie Chaplin's genius was in comedy. He had no sense of humour, particularly about himself.

Lita Grey, his ex-wife

If you can't see the humour in yourself, you could be missing the joke of the century.

Dame Edna Everage

TRAVEL & COUNTRIES

TRAVEL & TOURISM

When one realizes that his life is worthless he either commits suicide or travels.

Edward Dahlberg

I think that travel comes from some deep urge to see the world, like the urge that brings up a worm in an Irish bog to see the moon when it is full.

Lord Dunsany

People travel to faraway places to watch, in fascination, the kind of people they ignore at home.

Dagobert D. Runes

One never feels such distaste for one's countrymen and countrywomen as when one meets them abroad.

Rose Macaulay

We can go away right now. I pack light. Everything we need is right here in my pants.

Ryan Harrison, to Lauren Goodhue, *Wrongfully Accused*

STREETS FLOODED. PLEASE ADVISE.

Robert Benchley, telegram sent on his arrival in Venice

Come on in here and see our stuff, señorita! We rip you off less!

Junk-Jewellery Seller, Tijuana market, overheard by Tee

I reckon that Stonehenge was built by the contemporary equivalent of Microsoft, whereas Avebury was definitely an Apple circle.

Terry Pratchett

Nepal is the most fun place in the world. You've got monkeys roaming around, cremations and animal sacrifices... The country could have been invented by Beavis and Butt-head. Even the gods have nice breasts.

Emo Philips

—You know what I want to get while I'm here in India? A Sherpa. That would be so cool.
—What's a Sherpa?
—It's, like, a people endemic to the Himalayas. You can buy one, and they carry your stuff for you!

Two American Girls in Goa, India,
overheard by wish I were Canadian

The tyrannical beauty of Hawaii, after a little while, becomes a little troubling. The beauty, the palm trees... It's like being hit over the head with a rainbow.

Russell Brand

Any sizable Portuguese town looks like a superstitious bride's finery – something old, something new, something borrowed, and something blue.

Mary McCarthy

Some years ago entering Stonehenge, I overheard a harassed mother say to her small daughter, 'Now, just you be careful and don't knock anything over.'

L. Markes

Asthmatics: avoid going on holiday to places where the scenery is described as breathtaking.

Top Tip, *Viz* magazine

Fortissimo at last!

Gustav Mahler, visiting Niagara Falls

Niagara Falls would be more impressive if it flowed the other way.

Oscar Wilde

I had this great idea to make the Great Wall of China into a handball court.

George Gobel

Noël Coward was once staying round the corner from the Taj Mahal and refused to see it. 'I'd seen it on biscuit boxes and didn't want to spoil the illusion.'

John Heilpern

Ruins, museums and cathedrals...leave no imprint whatsoever. In fact, many of the world's noblest antiquities have definitely irritated me. Perhaps the sheen on them of so many hundreds of years' intensive appreciation makes them smug.

Noël Coward

As for seeing the town, he did not even think of it, being of that breed of Britons who have their servants do their sightseeing for them.

Jules Verne, *Around the World in Eighty Days*

He who has seen one cathedral ten times has seen something; he who has seen ten cathedrals once has seen but little; and he who has spent half an hour in each of a hundred cathedrals has seen nothing at all.

Sinclair Lewis

Like all great travellers, I have seen more than I remember, and remember more than I have seen.

Benjamin Disraeli

Most of my treasured memories of travel are recollections of sitting.
Robert Thomas Allen

In Paris they just simply...stared when we spoke to them in French! We never did succeed in making those idiots understand their own language.

Mark Twain

Why do you want to go Paris? There are parts of Reading you haven't seen yet.

Eva Gervais, to her son, Ricky

Travelling is the ruin of all happiness! There's no looking at a building here, after seeing Italy.

Fanny Burney

—I just heard General de Gaulle has died. I wonder what he and

God are talking about in heaven?
—That depends on how good God's French is.

Friend and Noël Coward

A blade of grass is always a blade of grass, whether in one country or another.

Dr Samuel Johnson, preferring people-watching to views

Do you know, if you took all the metal that it took to make the Eiffel Tower and laid it end to end...it would fall down.

Sandi Toksvig

—Coming up?
—What's up there?
—The view.
—The view of what? The view of down here? I can see that down here.
—Ray, you are about the worst tourist in the whole world.

Ken and Ray, *In Bruges*

I'm 73 years old, I've seen half the wonders of the world and I never laid eyes on a finer sight than the curve of Betty Browning's breasts.

Grandfather George, *Hope and Glory*

AMERICA

I am willing to love all mankind, except an American.

Dr Samuel Johnson

America: 20 Million Illegal Immigrants Can't Be Wrong!

Richard Jeni, slogan against anti-Americanism

I came to America because I heard the streets were paved with gold. When I got here I found out three things. First, they weren't paved with gold; second, they weren't paved at all; and third, I was expected to pave them.

Italian Immigrant, in a letter to his relatives, 1912

America is a place where Jewish merchants sell Zen love beads to

Agnostics for Christmas.

John Burton Brimer

Americans may have no identity, but they do have wonderful teeth.

Jean Baudrillard

My niece married a Greek who had taken out his US naturalization papers, and was very proud of his new status. They recently purchased a home; and when the deed came, he looked it over solemnly, then grinned and broke into a little dance step. 'I'm a real American now,' he exclaimed, 'I'm in debt!'

R.M. Fee

The American way is the way most law-abiding, tax-paying Americans live – in debt. Does this make a balanced budget un-American?

Cullen Hightower

Un-American: wicked, intolerable, heathenish.

Ambrose Bierce

A Coke is a Coke and no amount of money can get you a better Coke than the one the bum on the corner is drinking. All the Cokes are the same and all the Cokes are good… The idea of America is so wonderful because the more equal something is, the more American it is.

Andy Warhol

In the United States there is more space where nobody is than where anybody is. That is what makes America what it is.

Gertrude Stein

Nothing that you say about the whole country is going to be true.

Alistair Cooke

America is a vast conspiracy to make you happy.

John Updike

The American people never carry an umbrella. They prepare to walk in eternal sunshine.

Alfred E. Smith

The happy ending is our national belief.

Mary McCarthy

If America leads a blessed life, then why did God put all of our oil under people who hate us?

Jon Stewart

Double – no triple – our troubles and we'd still be better off than any other people on earth.

Ronald Reagan

Asked if they think they are good at maths, Americans tend to answer yes when they are not, while Koreans answer no when they are.

Alan Wolfe

The British think they have a sense of irony. They also think they have a special relationship with America. But they cannot have it both ways.

Miles Kington

We are all American at puberty; we die French.

Evelyn Waugh

AUSTRALIA

The land that foreplay forgot.

Germaine Greer

Australia is still a male-chauvinist bastion and most of the women like it that way.

Paul Hogan

In Australia, not reading poetry is the national pastime.

Phyllis McGinley

Never do business with an Australian who says 'no worries' a lot.

Frank Moorhouse

CANADA

What a place, Canada! They started a country and no one showed up.

Wally Sparks, *Meet Wally Sparks*

Canada is like a loft apartment over a really great party. Like, 'Keep it down, eh?'

Robin Williams

The most parochial nationette on earth.

Wyndham Lewis

A Canadian is somebody who knows how to make love in a canoe.

Pierre Berton

I have to spend so much time explaining to Americans that I am not English and to Englishmen that I am not American that I have little time left to be Canadian.

Laurence J. Peter

Americans are benevolently ignorant about Canada, while Canadians are malevolently well informed about the United States.

J. Bartlet Brebner

In the world menu, Canada must be considered the vichyssoise of nations – it's cold, half-French and difficult to stir.

Stuart Keate

I don't like living any place where I'm older than the buildings.

Joe Grundy, *The Archers*

The tragedy of Canada is that they had the opportunity to have French cuisine, British culture, and American technology, and instead they ended up with British cuisine, American culture, and French technology.

Will Shetterly, *overheard*

GREAT BRITAIN
– GENERAL

The British have three qualities: humour, tenacity and realism.
I sometimes think we are still at the humour stage.

Georges Pompidou

Being British is about driving in a German car to an Irish pub
where we imbibe copious amounts of Belgian or eastern European
beer, then on the way home stopping to pick up an Indian curry or
a Turkish kebab to consume as we sit on our Swedish furniture
watching American shows on Japanese TVs.

Robert Readman

We have all got to be as British as Carry On films and scotch eggs
and falling over on the beach while trying to change into your
swimming trunks with a towel on. We should all feel the same
mysterious pang at the sight of the Queen.

Boris Johnson

Does anyone else feel a tinge of British pride when they see people
drinking pints of lager in the airport before it's turned 8am?

Richard Bacon

The passion to be left alone, if only to one's own foolishness, lies
deep rooted in the British character.

Stephen Leacock

ENGLAND

In order to appreciate England one has to have a certain contempt
for logic.

Lin Yutang

We do not regard Englishmen as foreigners. We look on them only
as rather mad Norwegians.

Halvard Lange, Norwegian politician

You can go sauntering along for a certain period, telling the English some interesting things about themselves, and then all at once it feels as if you have stepped on the prongs of a rake.

Patrick Campbell

I'm American... but I live in England with my English husband. By that I mean he eats pizza with a knife and fork. And sunburns under a 50-watt bulb.

Kit Hollerbach

It is, of course, a particularly British characteristic to think that every man is the same under the skin, and that Eskimos are really only would-be Old Etonians wearing fur coats.

John Harvey-Jones

He was born in Luton or, as EasyJet call it, London.

David Mitchell, *The Unbelievable Truth*

London, that *hot-plate* of humanity, on which we first sing, then simmer, then boil, then dry away to dust.

Thomas Hardy

That slowest and dreariest of boroughs...where the inhabitants are driven to ring their own door-bells lest they should rust from disuse.

Ouida, on Cantitborough (modelled on Bury St Edmunds)

Sir Clement Freud wanted to call a horse Bury St Edmunds but the local council turned it down. He called it Digup St Edmunds instead.

Michael Chapman

I spent a year in that town, one Sunday.

Warwick Deeping

The beautiful thing about Brighton is that you can buy your lover a pair of knickers at Victoria Station and have them off again at the Grand Hotel in less than two hours.

Keith Waterhouse

My apologies to the citizens of Chipping Sodbury for calling their town Chipping Sudbury last week. Fact is always stranger than fiction.

Stephen Glover

M3, car park, car park, roundabout, car park, roundabout, car park, tart, roundabout, M3.

Andy, on a drive through Basingstoke, *Crap Towns*

According to legend, Telford is so dull that the bypass was built before the town.

Victor Lewis-Smith

Jade went to Newcastle to do a film premiere and she went, 'Do I need euros, Mum?'

Jackiey Budden, on Jade Goody

I would never leave England. I am too fond of complaining about the government.

Julian Fellowes

He was inordinately proud of England and he abused her incessantly.

H.G. Wells

IRELAND

I am not an American, but I am the next worst thing – an Irishman.

George Bernard Shaw

A nation of masturbators under priestly instruction.

Brian Moore, *Fergus*

Ireland remains a deeply religious country, with the two main denominations being 'us' and 'them'.

Frank McNally

When I was in primary school we had a drawing on the wall of Northern Ireland with blue surrounding it. I thought Northern Ireland was an island until I was 12.

Anne Dunlop

I know I've got Irish blood because I wake up every day with a hangover.

Noel Gallagher

The famous drinking exists largely as material for anecdotes...
The conversation hardly leaves a man time to swallow anything.

Wilfred Sheed

An Irishman will always soften bad news, so that a...near-hurricane
that leaves thousands homeless is 'good drying weather'.

Hugh Leonard

If one could only teach the English how to talk and the Irish how
to listen, society here would be quite civilized.

Oscar Wilde

SCOTLAND

Want to know what the world will be like after the Apocalypse?
Four pounds on National Express gets you to Glasgow.

Jimmy Carr, *8 Out Of 10 Cats*

That garret of the earth – that knuckle-end of England – that land
of Calvin, oatcakes and sulphur.

Rev. Sydney Smith

Get yer haggis, right here! Chopped heart and lungs boiled in a wee
sheep's stomach. Tastes as good as it sounds.

Groundskeeper Willie, *The Simpsons*

I think most Scottish cuisine is based on a dare.

Charlie Mackenzie, *So I Married an Axe Murderer*

—Scotland is a very vile country to be sure.
—Well, Sir! God made it.
—Certainly he did, but we must always remember that he made it
for Scotchmen.

Dr Samuel Johnson and Mr Strahan

You must not look down on...Glasgow which gave the world the
internal combustion engine, political economy, antiseptic and
cerebral surgery, the balloon, the mariner's compass, the theory of
Latent Heat, Tobias Smollett and James Bridie.

James Bridie

The Scots are a very tough people. They have drive-by headbuttings. In Glasgow a sweatband is considered a silencer.

Emo Philips

Some place, Govan, eh? Where else can you get a fish supper at 9am? Simple, just steal it off a drunk that's been lyin' pished outside a close all night.

Rab C. Nesbitt

The most Scottish thing I've ever seen: I was going through a town called Bathgate at about half past eleven at night, and there was a guy pissing against a front door. He then took out his keys and went inside.

Frankie Boyle, *Mock the Week*

Glasgow is not a melting pot; it's closer to a chip pan in which you've attempted to boil cream, the ingredients have separated, and neither element is palatable.

Tom Lappin

For a while I did unite the Rangers and Celtic fans. There were people in both camps who hated me.

Mo Johnston, Scottish striker who played with both football teams

It's been said that Scotland is an argument. That's so true. It's where the enlightenment came from.

Elaine Smith

I think it possible that all Scots are illegitimate, Scotsmen being so mean and Scotswomen so generous.

Edwin Muir

If you unscotch us, you will find us damned mischievous Englishmen.

Sir Walter Scott

God help England if she had no Scots to think for her!

George Bernard Shaw

I went to Scotland and found nothing there that looks like Scotland.

Arthur Freed, on why the film *Brigadoon*
was shot in MGM studios in Hollywood

The noblest prospect which a Scotsman ever sees is the high road that leads him to England!

Dr Samuel Johnson

WALES

What do you call a sheep tied to a lamp post in Cardiff? A leisure centre. No, no, don't laugh! It's an example of the institutionalized racism against the Welsh!

Rob Brydon, *QI*

First God made England, Ireland and Scotland. That's when he corrected his mistakes and made Wales.

Katharine Hepburn

Show a Welshman a dozen exits, one of which is marked 'Self-Destruction', and he will go right through that door.

Joseph L. Mankiewicz, after directing Richard Burton in *Cleopatra*

All the Welsh are natural actors. Only the bad ones become professionals.

Richard Burton

Welsh rain...descends with the enthusiasm of someone breaking bad news.

Saki

The Welsh are the Italians in the rain.

Anon

It was...controversially asked, 'What are the Welsh for?' I was brought up to believe that our purpose in God's scheme of things was to keep the Irish and the English apart.

Michael Bissmire

SCIENCE & TECHNOLOGY

COMPUTER

I think I bought a bad computer. The mouse bit me.

David Letterman

My Apple Mac is so high-tech it can do everything. I'm frightened to press a button in case I launch a space shuttle.

Kathy Lette

—How much should my computer cost?
—About $350 less than you will actually pay.

Dave Barry

There are only two industries that refer to their customers as 'users'.

Edward Tufte

User: the word that computer professionals use when they mean 'idiot'.

Dave Barry

Those parts of the system that you can hit with a hammer are called 'hardware'; those program instructions that you can only curse at are called software.

Anon

There is only one satisfying way to boot a computer.

J.H. Goldfuss

I always refer to any machine I work on as 'Annie'. This was the name of my first girlfriend. She was equally ungiving and unforgiving.

David P. Lintott

Don't anthropomorphize computers. They hate it.

Anon

I believe in the total depravity of inanimate things.

Katherine Kent Child Walker

The nice thing about Windows is, it does not just crash, it displays a dialog box and let's you press 'OK' first.

Arno Shaefer

Jesus saves! The rest of us better make backups.

Anon

I took a two-year-old computer in to be repaired, and the guy looked at me as though he was a gun dealer and I had brought him a musket. In just two years, I'd gone from cutting-edge to Amish.

Jon Stewart

It would take one hundred clerks working for one hundred years to make a mistake as monumental as a single computer can make in one thousandth of a second.

Dental Economics magazine

They've finally come up with the perfect office computer. If it makes a mistake, it blames another computer.

Milton Berle

Computers make it easier to do a lot of things, but most of the things they make it easier to do don't need to be done.

Andy Rooney

Our new computer system is about as much use as a cat flap in a submarine.

Unidentified Employee at Tory HQ

Computers aren't very intelligent. On the evolutionary scale, they're on the same level as a sea-slug.

Computer Programmer

The computer was working fine when Rob started; after several hours of installation, it was a totally dysfunctional, muttering, potentially violent thing, and we had to take it outside and shoot it.

Dave Barry

Never trust a computer you can't throw out of a window.

Stephen Wozniak

The cause of the problem in 97.3 per cent of cases is a simple fault with the nut attached to the keyboard.

Steve Turner

This granny finds that spending ten hours a week on the keyboard helps to sustain and even improve one's waning powers of concentration, muscular co-ordination, aural attention, critical self-appraisal, finger dexterity and musical appreciation. The instrument in question is called a pianoforte.

Pauline M. Atkins

INTERNET

—Behold... the Internet.
—My God! It's full of ads!

Bender and Philip J. Fry, *Futurama*

I bought a novelty hot water bottle on Amazon for Christmas and in Amazon's infinite wisdom they suggested I buy an Andrea Bocelli CD to go with it.

Dan H., online shopper

The Internet is just a world passing around notes in a classroom.

Jon Stewart

The Internet: Transforming Society and Shaping the Future Through Chat.

Dave Barry

You can't define 'news' on the Web since everyone with a homepage is a global town crier.

Joshua Quittner

My little sister got me on Facebook because I was on MySpace... So I joined both. But I keep muddling them up, so I keep asking people to come on MyFace. Still, 80,000 friends...

Shappi Khorsandi

The trouble with the global village is all the global village idiots.
Paul Ginsparg

The Internet: absolute communication, absolute isolation.
Paul Carvel

I've joined an *anti*-social networking site. It's called
Shutyerfacebook.

Anon

Too many twits might make a twat.
David Cameron, on Twitter

I think I'll live to see the end of capital letters.
**Larry Gelbart, on the 21st century preference for
using lower-case letters in email and on the Web**

The Internet is not, actually, very much like a private
correspondence which will be read by the addressee only. It is more
like standing in the street, naked, shouting random secrets, forever.
Philip Hensher

You can't take something off the Internet – it's like taking pee out
of a pool.

Anon

Computers can now keep a man's every transgression recorded in a
permanent memory bank, duplicating with complex programming
and intricate wiring a feat his wife handles quite well without fuss
or fanfare.

Lane Olinghouse

It all boils down to just a bunch of ones and zeroes. I don't know
how that enables me to see naked women, but however it works, God
bless you guys.
Doug Heffernan, *The King of Queens*

Well, thanks to the Internet, I'm now bored with sex.
Philip J. Fry, *Futurama*

EVOLUTION & CREATIONISM

That ugly beast the ape's the very spit of us!
Quintus Ennius (c.239–169 BC)

How extremely stupid not to have thought of that!
Thomas Huxley, on first reading *The Origin of Species* by Charles Darwin

Ah, Corporal Klinger, my constant reminder that Darwin was right.
Major Charles Winchester, *M*A*S*H*

According to archaeologists, for millions of years Neanderthal man was not fully erect. That's easy to understand considering how ugly Neanderthal women were.

Anon

We have reason to believe that Man first walked upright to free his hands for masturbation.

Lily Tomlin

To introduce creationism into schools as a counterbalance to evolution would be like introducing the stork as a counterbalance to the study of conception, pregnancy and childbirth.

Brian P. Block

Science has proof without any certainty. Creationists have certainty without any proof.

Ashley Montagu, *attrib*.

TIME

The shortest perceptible slice of time is the ohnosecond: that infinitely painful moment between shutting the front door and realizing that your keys are still inside the house.

David Colvin

—What's the definition of an eternity?
—The time from when you come to when she leaves.

Anon

God, who winds up our sundials...

Georg Christoph Lichtenberg

I have a *carpe diem* mug and, truthfully, at six in the morning the words do not make me want to seize the day. They make me want to slap a dead poet.

Joanne Sherman

A femtosecond is a millionth of a billionth of a second... Put in comparative terms, a femtosecond is to a second as a second is to 32 million years.

Professor Ahmed Zewail

The femtosecond may be defined as the interval between the traffic light changing to green and the person in the vehicle behind sounding their horn.

John Thurston

The femtosecond is the time it takes for the smile to leave the face of an airline's chief flight attendant as he walks from Club Class to Economy Class.

John Bell

In our house, the femtosecond denoted the time which elapsed between putting on a fresh nappy, and its being filled by a grateful, gurgling infant.

Kieran Sweeney

For cruciverbalists...a femtosecond is the interval between a clue being utterly obscure and blindingly obvious.

Stanley Armstrong

In my street the shortest space of time is that between a car leaving a parking space and another occupying it.

Evan M. Davies

There is never enough time unless you're serving it.

Malcolm Forbes

The shortest recorded period of time lies between the minute you put some money away for a rainy day and the unexpected arrival of rain.

Jane Bryant Quinn

MATHEMATICS

—How are you at mathematics?
—I speak it like a native.

Moriarty and Secombe, *The Goon Show*

One plus one is two. Two plus two is four. But five will get you ten if you know how to work it.

Mae West

There are three kinds of mathematicians: those who can count and those who cannot.

Anon

—How many grains of sand in the Sahara, then, d'you reckon?
—I lost count. It's quite a few. I got up to 17 and it's definitely more than that.

Alan Davies and Stephen Fry, *QI*

Round numbers are always false.

Dr Samuel Johnson

Five out of four people have trouble with fractions.

Steven Wright

G.H. Hardy, who was professor of pure mathematics...told me once that if he could find a proof that I was going to die in five minutes he would of course be sorry to lose me, but this sorrow would be quite outweighed by pleasure in the proof. I entirely sympathized with him and was not at all offended.

Bertrand Russell

Dreamt I solved the Poincaré Conjecture using a tennis racket, a teapot and a rubber sheet. It really worked but vital steps gone.

Stephen Fry

I'm not very good with diagrams. I remember when I first saw the one in the Lil-lets packet...I thought, no, I'll just put a ship in a bottle each month, it'll be quicker.

Victoria Wood

Paralllels.

Professor Robert C. Art

Do not worry about your difficulties in mathematics; I can assure you that mine are still greater.

Albert Einstein

INVENTIONS

The printing press is either the greatest credit or the greatest curse of modern times, one sometimes forgets which.

J.M. Barrie

Some sad news from Australia... the inventor of the boomerang grenade died today.

Johnny Carson

I ran into Isosceles. He has a great idea for a new triangle!

Woody Allen

Do you suppose the inventor of the vibrator heard a voice that said: 'If you build it, they will come.'

Anon

—All you have to do is think of things which people need but which don't exist yet...or you could take something that already exists and find a new use for it, like—
—Hamburger earmuffs!

Professor Frink and Homer Simpson, *The Simpsons*

Probably the earliest fly swatters were nothing more than some sort of striking surface attached to the end of a long stick.

Jack Handey

What a lucky thing the wheel was invented before the automobile; otherwise, can you imagine the awful screeching?

Samuel Hoffenstein

Anything invented after you're 35 is against the natural order of things.

Douglas Adams

I would have preferred to invent something which helps people. A lawnmower, for example.

Mikhail Kalashnikov, inventor of the AK-47 assault rifle

—What use is electricity?
—Why, sir, there is every possibility that you will soon be able to tax it!

William Ewart Gladstone and Michael Faraday, physicist

Thomas Edison spent years trying to invent the electric light... Finally, late one night, he got the bulb to glow. He ran out of his laboratory, through the house, up the stairs to his bedroom. 'Honey,' Edison called to his wife, 'I've done it!' She rolled over and said, 'Will you turn that light off and come to bed!'

Ron Dentinger

ASTRONOMY

The universe is merely a fleeting idea in God's mind – a pretty uncomfortable thought, particularly if you've just made a down payment on a house.

Woody Allen

In the beginning, there was nothing. God said, 'Let there be light.' And there was light. There was still nothing, but you could see it much better.

Ellen DeGeneres

The origin of the universe was, of course, the Big Bang, which happened about 14,700 billion years ago. I was away at the time.

Patrick Moore

—What existed before the Big Bang?
—That is like asking what is north of the North Pole. It is a meaningless question.
—Well I've asked a few of those in my time.

Richard Madeley and Professor Stephen Hawking

Being stuck between Rugby and Nuneaton in a broken-down train is bad enough. Being lost in space is probably marginally worse.

Michael Fabricant, on Virgin's plans to expand into space tourism

Space is only 80 miles from every person on earth – far closer than most people are to their own national capitals.

Daniel Deudney

We have a few clues as to what space smells like… Astronauts reported a smell of fried steak, hot metal and even welding a motorbike.

Steven Pearce

For years politicians have promised the moon. I'm the first one to be able to deliver it.

President Richard Nixon, *attrib*., on the first moon landing, 1969

—Forget the moon. Everybody goes to the moon. We'll go to the sun.
—We can't go to the sun. If we get within 13 million miles of it, we'll melt.
—So we go at night.

Two Aspiring Astronauts

The sun? That's the hottest place on Earth!

Homer Simpson

—Landing cameras on Mars is like hitting a hole in one, only you start in California and end in Australia…
—…and Australia's moving!

Two Scientists, on the Mars Polar Lander project

The Mars Polar Lander has been quieter than George W. Bush after a foreign policy question.

David Letterman, when the space exploration vehicle went missing in outer space

Put three grains of sand inside a vast cathedral, and the cathedral will be more closely packed with sand than space is with stars.

Sir James Jeans

There are more stars in the universe than there have ever been heartbeats in the whole of humankind.

**Fact learned on a visit to the Royal Observatory,
Greenwich, noted by Paul Milligan**

[*gazing at the stars in the sky*] Let's go inside and watch television. I'm beginning to feel insignificant.

Charlie Brown

SOCIETY & LAW

CLASS

An Englishman's social standing seems to depend on the number of people he can afford to despise.

Peter McArthur

Let me explain the order of things to you: there's the aristocracy, the upper class, the middle class, working class, dumb animals, waiters, creeping things, head lice, people who eat packet soup, then you.

Gareth Blackstock, *Chef!*

Put three Englishmen on a desert island and within an hour they'll have invented a class system.

Alan Ayckbourn

The English are like their beer: froth at the top, dregs at the bottom, and excellent in the middle.

Voltaire

The middle classes are rancid scraps in the middle of the luscious, bad-for-you bread of British life.

Julie Burchill

The middle classes will kill football. The middle classes kill everything they touch.

Matthew Parris

The only class you do *not* belong to and are not proud of at all is the lower-middle class. No one ever describes himself as belonging to the lower-middle class.

George Mikes

By and large, I've met a better class of person in the gutter than I have in the drawing room.

Jeffrey Bernard

You might be a redneck if...when your wife left you, she took the house with her; you take your dog for a walk and you both use the tree at the corner; you've ever unstopped a sink with a shotgun; you've ever worn a tube-top to a funeral home; you work with a shirt off... and so does your husband.

Jeff Foxworthy

In life there exist two classes: first class and no class.

Hugh Leonard

ROYALTY

Imagine the Queen meeting Camilla. 'You're my son's mistress? That must be interesting.'

Linda Smith, *I Think the Nurses are Stealing my Clothes*

Pat Boone met the Queen at a Royal Variety Performance. She said to him: 'We've met before, haven't we?' He said: 'Have we?'

Maureen Lipman

I only met the Queen briefly, at a party for World War II veterans, but I remember noticing what a good bra she was wearing.

Barbara Windsor

I met the Queen years ago at a Megastars Anonymous meeting. She was a quiet little thing in the corner with a little scarf over her tiara. I recognized her jewellery. My butler had sold it to her.

Dame Edna Everage

Former royal butler Paul Burrell – facially, a cross between Jamie Oliver and a simpering broad bean.

Charlie Brooker

Prince Philip is a bloody-minded man with a temper as foul as an arthritic corgi.

Jean Rook

I remember asking Diana who were the people she admired most in the world. She named three: Margaret Thatcher, Mother Teresa and Madonna.

Andrew Morton

It was the usual 'zoo tea'. You know, we eat – the others watch.
Princess Margaret, at a public reception

The food was memorable. Tiny fragments of nouvelle cuisine, everything tastefully decorated with crossed chives. I obviously stopped at McDonald's, Wandsworth, on the way home.
Charles Saatchi, dining at Windsor Castle with
Prince Charles, *Charles Saatchi: Question*

I just didn't know what to do with the little bag.
Prince Charles, explaining to President Ronald Reagan
why he didn't drink the cup of tea served to him at the
White House, which contained a teabag

—How do you manage to act charming and not look bored at everyone's questions?
—A thousand years of breeding.
Questioner in New York and Prince Charles

To be Prince of Wales is not a position. It is a predicament.
Prince of Wales, *The Madness of King George*

Nobody but me can possibly understand how perfectly bloody it is to be Prince of Wales.
Prince Charles

We're all in line to succession to the throne. If 48 million people die, I shall become Queen.
Peter Cook

—Lord St John of Fawsley refuses to acknowledge the Royal Family are ever wrong about anything. If the Queen was found to practise cannibalism, the noble lord would fatten up a missionary in his back garden for her.
—No, I would offer myself as the main course.
Dr Piers Brendon and Lord St John of Fawsley

I'm doing pretty well considering. In the past, when anyone left the
Royal family they had you beheaded.

Sarah Ferguson, Duchess of York

ARISTOCRACY

Take a good look: there are only 24 of these in the country.

**The Duke of Marlborough, to an interested party
at the urinals of his gentleman's club**

A title is really rather a nuisance in these democratic days. As
George Hartford I had everything I wanted. Now I have merely
everything other people want, which isn't nearly so pleasant.

Lord Illingworth, *A Woman of No Importance*

I was once naive enough to ask the late Duke of Devonshire why
he liked Eastbourne and he replied with a self-deprecating shrug
that one of the things he liked was that he owned it.

A.N. Wilson

[*filling out an official form*]
Q: How long has your family lived at the present address?
A: 697 years.

Sir Thomas Ingilby, of Ripley Castle

I believe in inherited wealth. Society needs to have some people
who are above it all.

Edward Digby Baltzell

The strength of England is that they have no real aristocracy.
Anyone's blood can become blue for a lump sum down.

Nancy Astor

One has often wondered whether upon the whole earth there is
anything so unintelligent, so unapt to perceive how the world is
really going, as an ordinary young Englishman of our upper class.

Matthew Arnold

There is always more brass than brains in an aristocracy.

Oscar Wilde

To discard magnificence, and remain magnificent, is the inimitable privilege of aristocracy.

Falconer Madan

In England, having had money…is just as acceptable as having it, since the upper-class mannerisms persist, even after the bankroll has disappeared. But never having had money is unforgivable, and can only be atoned for by never trying to get any.

Margaret Halsey

Did you know that a peer condemned to death had the right to be hanged with a silken cord? A bit like insisting that the electric chair had to be Chippendale.

Charles Mosley

CLASS CONSCIOUSNESS

A lobster and a crab fell in love and wished to marry but the lobster's mother disapproved: 'Crabs are common, and what is more, they walk *sideways*!' 'Just meet him, Mother,' begged the lobster. She brought in the crab who walked in a perfectly straight line to greet the lobster's mother. 'But I thought crabs always walked sideways,' she said. 'They do,' replied the crab, 'but I'm drunk.'

Anon

Could someone please settle this: in a Rolls-Royce Corniche the bar opens from *left* to *right,* doesn't it?

Sylvia Pickel, *Vibes*

He's so snobbish he won't even travel in the same car as his chauffeur.

David Frost

I went to a party given for Noël Coward, and at those parties everybody tries to act so British. There was a dame there riding a Kotex sidesaddle.

Jack Benny

There is no snob like a left-wing snob.

Andrew Neil

Good Lord, I can't believe I'm at a public pool. Why doesn't someone just pee on me directly?

Karen Walker, *Will and Grace*

I never look at price labels. Someone once told me it was common. That and sending mixed-coloured flowers.

Julie Burchill

Having photographs around the house is fine – if they're royal and on the piano.

Nicky Haslam, interior designer

Before God and the bus driver we are all equal.

German proverb

LAW & LAWYERS

In the past when I've talked to audiences like this, I've often started off with a lawyer joke, a caricature of a lawyer who's been nasty, greedy and unethical. But I've stopped that practice. I gradually realized that the lawyers in the audience didn't think the jokes were funny and the non-lawyers didn't know they were jokes.

Chief Justice William Rehnquist, making a speech

—How many lawyers does it take to change a light bulb?
—How many can you afford?

Anon

Ninety-nine per cent of all lawyers give the rest a bad name.

Anon

You've heard about the man who got the bill from his lawyer, which said: 'For crossing the road to speak to you and discovering it was not you: $12.'

George S. Kaufman

And God said: 'Let there be Satan, so people don't blame everything on me. And let there be lawyers, so people don't blame everything on Satan.'

George Burns

—You're a lawyer?
—I prefer 'law stylist'.

Liz Lemon and Floyd, *30 Rock*

I didn't become a lawyer because I like the law. The law sucks. It's boring, but it can also be used as a weapon. You want to bankrupt somebody? Cost him everything he's worked for? Make his wife leave him, even make his kids cry... yeah, we can do that.

Richard Fish, *Ally McBeal*

Lawyers and tarts are the two oldest professions in the world. And we always aim to please.

Horace Rumpole, *Rumpole of the Bailey*

A lawyer is one who protects you against robbers by taking away the temptation.

H.L. Mencken

A peasant between two lawyers is like a fish between two cats.

Spanish proverb

Apologists for the profession contend that lawyers are as honest as other men, but this is not very encouraging.

Ferdinand Lundberg

If you can think about a thing that is inextricably attached to something else without thinking of the thing which it is attached to, then you have a legal mind.

Thomas Reed Powell

Now I realise what Mark Twain meant when he said, 'The more you explain it, the more I don't understand it.'

Justice Robert H. Jackson

One listens to one's lawyer prattle on as long as one can stand it and then signs where indicated.

Alexander Woollcott

I think the reason justice is blind is because lawyers are jerking off all the time.

Dennis Miller

I decided law was the exact opposite of sex: even when it was good it was lousy.

Mortimer Zuckerman

CRIME

Fellow walked up to me and said: 'You see a cop around here?' I said, 'No.' He said, 'Stick 'em up!'

Henny Youngman

Thieves! Thieves... O pray, sir, spare all I have, and take my life!

George Farquhar

I came from a pretty tough neighbourhood. Nothing but killings. I went out and bought a water bed – and there was a guy at the bottom of it.

Joey Adams

You think New York is bad? You ought to go to Detroit. You can go ten blocks and never leave the scene of the crime.

Red Skelton

New Orleans is the only city in the world you go in to buy a pair of nylon stockings and they want to know your head size.

Billie Holiday

When I approached the check-out counter of a Miami store, the clerk said, 'Cash, cheque or stick-up?'

Pat Williams

—What goes clip clop, clip clop, bang bang, clip clop, clip clop?
—An Amish drive-by shooting.

Anon

—How do you explain this huge rise in crime?
—There's so much more to nick.

Interviewer and Douglas Hurd, MP

Nothing incites to money-crimes like great poverty or great wealth.

Mark Twain

Some guy came running in the other night and said, 'Somebody stole my car!' I said, 'Did you see him?' He said, 'No, but I got his licence number.'

Bill Barner

I used to leave a pair of dirty underpants on the driver's seat of my car because I always thought anybody wanting to steal the car would look in and think, 'Oh dear, oh dear, look at that. There's bound to be another one round the corner, we'll take that instead.'

John Peel

There is no such thing as an unexpectedly pleasant ring on your doorbell in London. The only people who ring when you don't expect it are the police, religious maniacs, menacing youths selling products that are undoubtedly criminally acquired, bailiffs and your in-laws.

Michael Gove, MP

In England, if you commit a crime, the police say, 'Stop! Or I'll say 'stop' again!'

Robin Williams

Figures released today by the FBI show that for the first time there is now as much crime on the streets as there is on TV.

Joey Adams

Growing up in inner London somewhere today, I would possibly have been a hoodie.

Norman Tebbit

—It isn't fair what people say about him. They'd tell you he'd sell his own mother. I heard that on very good authority.
—Who from?
—The two blokes who bought his mother.

Ingrid and Norman Stanley Fletcher, *Porridge*

Whenever he saw a dollar in another man's hands he took it as a personal grudge, if he couldn't take it any other way.

O. Henry

I like thieves. Some of my best friends are thieves. Why, just last week we had the president of the bank over for dinner.

W.C. Fields

What is robbing a bank compared with founding a bank?

Bertolt Brecht

—I would imagine the biggest problem in Uckfield is graffiti.
—It is. There's a river called the River Uck.

Nick Hancock and Contestant, *Duel,* **TV quiz**

Someone stole my identity. Now *he* has no life.

Larry Brown

'It restores your faith in natural justice,' said Pat McGillivray, of
Carisbrooke, after a snatch-thief grabbed her plastic carrier bag
which contained nothing more than the fresh droppings of Whisky,
Mrs McGillivray's West Highland terrier.

Isle of Wight County Press

A man in Illinois is suing a woman, claiming she stole his sperm to
have his baby without his knowledge. Now that's a good
pickpocket.

Conan O'Brien

—What's the difference between a pickpocket and a peeping Tom?
—A pickpocket snatches watches.

Redd Foxx

My ex-wife claimed she was violated. Knowing my ex-wife, it
wasn't a moving violation.

Woody Allen

Most paedophiles wear glasses and a beard. What is it about that
look that kids find so attractive?

Frankie Boyle

A Jewish child molester: 'Hey, kid…wanna buy some candy?'

Jackie Martling

—I'm going to kill you!
—Oh, John, *please* – mind your blood pressure.

John and Meg, *Salvation*

A first killing is like your first love. You never forget it.

Alexander Pichushkin, Russia's 'Chessboard Killer',
convicted of 48 murders

Do you know why it's so hard to solve a Redneck murder? Cos there's no dental records and all the DNA is the same.

Jeff Foxworthy

The criminal is the creative artist; the detective only the critic.

G.K. Chesterton

—How many cops does it take to throw a man down the stairs?
—None. He fell.

Anon

You know what I think is really wrong with the police in this country? Institutional sarcasm.

Frances Kapoor, *Criminal Justice*

If you really want to study police methods, do what I do: watch television.

Officer Gunther Toody, *Car 54, Where Are You?*

PRISON

Prison is like mime or juggling: a tragic waste of time.

Malcolm Hardee

Where would Christianity be if Jesus got 8 to 15 years, with time off for good behaviour?

James Donovan

The good thing about prison is that you never have to wonder what to wear.

Carol Siskind

Some zebras would love to sit behind bars if only to pretend they are white horses.

Stanislaw J. Lec

My prison would be walking through this world always having to listen to Eagles albums.

Kinky Friedman

—What do you call a clairvoyant midget who escaped from prison?
—A small medium at large.

Anon

HISTORY

I've gone back in time to when dinosaurs weren't just confined to zoos!

Homer Simpson

Stuff happens.

Donald Rumsfeld

I just adore history. It's so old.

Beulah (an American), *Romanoff and Juliet*

—If you could have dinner with anyone who lived in the history of the world, who would it be?
—That depends on the restaurant.

Interviewer and Rodney Dangerfield

I've always thought Alfred showed a marked lack of ingenuity over cakes – why didn't he cut off the burned bits, and ice the rest?

Madeleine Bingham

Tutankhamun looks like Tiger Woods eating a Cornetto.

Alan Davies, *QI*

J.P. Postgate was maintaining that the Roman Empire had to all intents everything we had. I asked whether they had asparagus (which we were eating). 'Oh yes.' 'What was it called?' 'Asparagus.'

John Edensor Littlewood

Twenty-two concubines, and a library of 62,000 volumes attested the variety of his inclinations, and from the productions which he left behind him, it appears that both the one and the other were designed for use rather than for ostentation.

Edward Gibbon, on Emperor Gordian the Younger

The best chance of reproducing the ancient Greek temperament
would be to cross the Scots with the Chinese.

Hugh MacDiarmid

After the death of Nelson, English ladies were fond of wearing the
Trafalgar garter, on which was inscribed the memorable signal:
'England expects every man to do his duty.'

Edmund Fuller

What if the French had successfully repelled the Germans in 1940?
They would have become a vainglorious, pompous, rude people
with a ridiculous sense of their importance in world affairs.

Jeff Chostner

—I slept through the 1960s.
—Don't worry, you didn't miss a thing.

Tennessee Williams and Gore Vidal

All the 'flower children' were as alike as a congress of accountants
and about as interesting.

John Mortimer

History repeats itself – the first time as tragi-comedy, the second
time as bedroom farce.

***Private Eye* magazine**

Those who don't study the past will repeat its errors; those who do
study it will find other ways to err.

Charles Wolf, Jr.

Any event, once it has occurred, can be made to appear inevitable
by a competent historian.

Lee Simonson

—What is the crucial virtue one requires of an historian – on or off
television – the single, unequivocal demand that we make?
—That he wears a leather jacket?

Charles Prentiss and Martin McCabe, *Absolute Power*

The only entirely creditable incident in English history is the
sending of £100 to Beethoven on his deathbed by the London
Philharmonic Society; and it is the only one that historians
never mention.

George Bernard Shaw

After you've heard two eyewitness accounts of a car accident, you begin to wonder about what passes for history.

H.R. Smith

WAR & PEACE

War is capitalism with the gloves off.

Tom Stoppard

I have never met anyone who wasn't against war. Even Hitler and Mussolini were, according to themselves.

Sir David Low

I detest war. It spoils armies.

Grand Duke Constantine of Russia

The belief in the possibility of a short decisive war appears to be one of the most ancient and dangerous of human illusions.

Robert Lynd

When you get into trouble 5,000 miles away from home, you've got to have been looking for it.

Will Rogers

Wars teach us not to love our enemies, but to hate our allies.

W.L. George

We should never fight a war unless we have been attacked and our country is in danger – or unless we are sure we can win.

Alex Ayres

You can no more win a war than you can win an earthquake.

Jeannette Rankin

The Romans never lost a war...because they never permitted a war to end until they won.

Louis D. Brandeis

All a soldier needs to know is how to shoot and salute.

General John Pershing

The only war where the men knew what they were fighting for was the Trojan War: it was fought over a woman.

William Lyon Phelps

Remember, gentlemen, it's not just France we are fighting for, it's Champagne!

Winston Churchill, 1918, during World War I

In war, you win or lose, live or die – and the difference is just an eyelash.

General Douglas MacArthur

You can be killed just as dead in an unjustified war as you can in one protecting your own home.

Will Rogers

At Victoria Station the RTO gave me a travel warrant, a white feather and a picture of Hitler marked 'This is your enemy'.
I searched every compartment but he wasn't on the train.

Spike Milligan, *Adolf Hitler, My Part in His Downfall*

Afghanistan is like you would imagine Colchester was like in Roman times.

Ray Winstone, 2009

Defence secretary, Geoff Hoon says that the city of Umm Qasr in Iraq is similar to Southampton. He's either never been to Southampton, or he's never been to Umm Qasr. There's no beer, no prostitutes and people are shooting at us. It's more like Portsmouth.

Unidentified British Soldier stationed in Iraq

I was at a field hospital in Basra. We went to speak to a squaddie who'd been blown up the day before, so I remarked: 'The only thing worse than being blown up on a Sunday is to be visited by politicians on a Monday,' to which he replied: 'Actually, it's on a par, sir.'

William Hague, in Iraq with David Cameron, 2006

You have to have a physical before you get into the army. A doctor looks in one ear, another doctor looks in the other ear, and if they can't see each other, you're in. And if they can see each other, you join the military police.

Joe E. Brown

Keep your bowels open, your mouth shut, and never volunteer.

Anon, advice to someone joining the army

Whenever I see a fellow look as if he was thinking, I say that's mutiny.

Sir Thomas Troubridge, naval commander

When I first went into the active army, you could tell someone to move a chair across the room. Now you have to tell him why.

Major Robert Lembke, 1979

There is only one way for a young man to get on in the army. He must try and get killed in every way he possibly can!

Sir Garnet Wolseley

When I lost my rifle, the army charged me $85. That's why in the navy, the captain goes down with the ship.

Dick Gregory

My brother just got out of the Marines. They made a man out of him. Paid for the operation and everything.

Stu Trivax

Women make better soldiers than men. They always know where the real enemy is hidden.

José Yglesias

In England, it is thought a good thing every now and then to shoot an admiral, to encourage the others.

Voltaire

The only thing more accurate than incoming enemy fire is incoming friendly fire.

Murphy's Military Law

The war situation has developed, not necessarily to Japan's advantage.

Emperor Hirohito, announcing Japan's surrender, 1945

A prisoner of war is a man who tries to kill you and fails, and then asks you not to kill him.

Winston Churchill

—Where was the soldier wounded?
—Ma'am, the bullet that wounded *him* would not have wounded *you*.

> **Unidentified Woman and Abraham Lincoln,**
> **during the American Civil War**

—Sometimes I ask myself how I'd stand up under torture.
—You kiddin'? If the Gestapo would take away your Bloomingdale's charge card, you'd tell 'em everything.

> **Annie Hall and Alvy Singer, *Annie Hall***

His brain has not only been washed, it has been dry-cleaned.

> **Dr Yen Lo, *The Manchurian Candidate***

If everyone demanded peace instead of another television set, then there'd be peace.

> **John Lennon**

Peace is what we call that brief moment between wars when people stop to reload.

> **James W. Dobson**

HEALTH MEDICINE & DRUGS

WEIGHT

I have the body of a man half my age. Unfortunately, he's in terrible shape.

George Foreman, aged 48

You're getting so big I need double vision to take you in.

Peter De Vries

I think one reason they call them 'Relaxed Fit' jeans is that 'Ass The Size of Texas' jeans would not sell very well.

Jim Rosenberg

Due to the recent heat wave, doctors are warning obese people to stay indoors. Not for their health, but because no one wants to see them in short pants.

Conan O'Brien

We're all concerned about your weight. Bart said NASA called. They said that your gravity is pulling all the satellites out of orbit.

Marge Simpson, to Homer

I won't tell you how much I weigh, but don't ever get in an elevator with me unless you're going down.

Jack E. Leonard

My life today is tough. My wife, she's attached to a machine that keeps her alive – the refrigerator.

Rodney Dangerfield

Come into the front parlour, and mind your hips on the ornaments – this hall can be very tricky for women of your build.

Pat Brandon, *I Didn't Know You Cared*

This girl was fat. I hit her with my car. She asked me, 'Why didn't you go around me?' I told her, 'I didn't have enough gas.'

Rodney Dangerfield

I hear they're going to tear you down and put up an office building where you're standing.

Groucho Marx

When you have a fat friend there are no see-saws. Only catapults.

Demetri Martin

She needs to lose thirty pounds or gain sixty. Anything in between has no place on television.

Jack Donaghy, about an actress, *30 Rock*

DIET

Diet: a system of starving yourself to death so you can live a little longer.

Totie Fields

I once drove with friends from Cannes to Nice. It took about an hour, and we dieted all the way.

Elsa Maxwell

According to a brand new scientific study, more than 90 per cent of diet plans used by Americans do not work. The American scientists conducted this study by looking out a window.

Conan O'Brien

I've written a diet book. It's called: 'Put That Down, Fatty.'

Jimmy Carr, *The Jonathan Ross Show*

You could lose a lot of weight if you'd just carry all your diet books around the block once a day.

Bill Hoest, cartoon caption

—How on earth do you keep that figure? Is it some special diet?
—No, lady, by isometric farting.

Gina Lollobrigida and Robert Mitchum

A great way to lose weight is to eat naked in front of the mirror. Restaurants will almost always throw you out before you can eat too much.

Frank Varano

Another good reducing exercise consists of placing both hands against the table edge and pushing back.

Robert Quillen

You can't survive by sucking the juice from a wet mitten.

Charles M. Schulz

Ah, Charles! I wish I were allowed even the wing of a roasted butterfly!

Rev. Sydney Smith

If one doesn't have a character like Abraham Lincoln or Joan of Arc, a diet simply disintegrates into eating exactly what you want to eat, but with a bad conscience.

Maria Augusta Trapp

I never worry about diets. The only carrots that interest me are the number you get in a diamond.

Mae West

Food is like sex: when you abstain, even the worst stuff begins to look good.

Beth McCollister

It is harder to eat sparingly than to fast. Moderation requires awareness. Renunciation requires only the tyranny of will.

Sandor McNab

The problem with food, of course, is that we can't ever really break up with it.

Cathy Guisewite

I'm so compulsive about losing weight, I weigh myself after I cough.

Elayne Boosler

Forget about calories – everything makes thin people thinner, and fat people fatter.

Mignon McLaughlin

Lord, if you can't make me thin – can you make all my friends fat?
Judy Hampton

—Is it true that you went on a diet that involved eating 9 eggs a day?
—Yes, it's true. I was fat and ugly and now I'm thin and ugly.
Questioner and Charles Saatchi,
My Name is Charles Saatchi and I am an Artoholic

Bulimia is still, to me, the number one eating disorder if you want a great body.

Brüno Gehard, aka Sacha Baron Cohen

If Mama Cass had shared her ham sandwich with Karen Carpenter, they'd both be alive today.

Anon

Loretta's losing 5 pounds a week on her new diet. I figure I'll be rid of her completely in about 10 months.

Bill Hoest, cartoon caption

If you hear of 16 or 18 pounds of human flesh, they belong to me. I look as if a curate had been taken out of me.

Rev. Sydney Smith, after losing weight

Even the soul has to go on a diet sometimes.

Stanislaw J. Lec

HEALTHY EATING

STEAKS, MARTINIS & CIGARS: YOU GOT A PROBLEM WITH THAT?

Restaurant sign, cartoon caption by Lee Lorenz

I'm allergic to food. Every time I eat, it breaks out in fat.
Jennifer Greene Duncan

I have a friend who's a macrobiotic. She doesn't eat meat, chicken, fish, white flour, sugar or preservatives. She can eat wicker.

Paula Poundstone

My whole family's lactose intolerant; when we take pictures we can't say 'Cheese'.

Jay London

All these disorders. When I was a kid we just had crazy people.

Ellen DeGeneres

If you are what you eat, no wonder most healthy eaters have the mentality of vegetables.

Julie Burchill

How do you get your children to avoid fatty, greasy, disgusting, unhealthy food? Don't let them eat from your plate.

Bill Dodds

I am opposed to refined, processed foods... If you were put into a can to be eaten 12 months later, how would you taste?

Yehudi Menuhin

Health Food: any food whose flavour is indistinguishable from that of the package in which it is sold.

Henry Beard

Tofu – what is that stuff? It's like chickpeas and grout. Food should not caulk windows.

Billiam Coronel

What is 'organic'? Just another word for dirty fruit.

Ruby Wax

People on a diet should have a salad dressing called '250 Islands'.

George Carlin

The only time to eat diet food is when you're waiting for the steak to cook.

Julia Child

Health nuts are going to feel stupid someday, lying in hospitals dying of nothing.

Redd Foxx

EXERCISE

Are you getting fit or having one?
Captain Benjamin 'Hawkeye' Pierce, *M*A*S*H*

Fitness experts are encouraging Americans to make small New Year's resolutions this year that they can keep, like adding five minutes to their exercise routines. As a result, most Americans will now have a five-minute exercise routine.

Conan O'Brien

The average American would drive his car to the bathroom if the doors were wide enough.

Anon

I won't say I'm out of condition now, but I even puff going downstairs.

Dick Gregory

I bought an exercise bicycle two years ago... the most expensive coat hanger in New York.

Robert Klein

If you are seeking creative ideas, go out walking. Angels whisper to a man when he goes for a walk.

Raymond Inmon

My beauty routine is a mixture of aerobics, isometrics and a little bit of yoga. To the observer it would look as if I was merely lifting a cup of coffee to my lips and lighting a cigarette.

Peter Cook

One time I said, 'You should jog around the block.' He said, 'Why? I'm already here.'

Phyllis Diller

All that running and exercise can do for you is make you healthy.
Denny McClain

For exercise, I wind my watch.

Robert Maxwell

A friend of mine runs marathons. He always talks about this 'runner's high'. But he has to go 26 miles for it. That's why I smoke and drink. I get the same feeling from a flight of stairs.

Larry Miller

Exercise is the most awful illusion. The secret is a lot of aspirin and *marrons glacés*.

Noël Coward

—Your body is the only home you'll ever have!
—Yes, my home is pretty messy. But I have a woman who comes in once a week.

Mr Universe and Johnny Carson

DENTIST

A Texas oil millionaire had toothache, so he went to the dentist and the dentist said: 'Where does it hurt?' The oil man replied, 'I feel lucky today – drill anywhere.'

Barry Took

Drill, fill and bill.

Newsweek magazine

The dentist told me I grind my teeth at night, so now before I go to sleep I fill my mouth with hot water and coffee beans and set my alarm for 7:30.

Jeff Marder

Simon Cowell's smile seems extra-dazzling – I can't tell if he's had his teeth whitened or his mouth blackened.

Peter Serafinowicz

—Root canal work is expensive. It'll come to $600.
—Six hundred dollars? Why don't you just add a toll bridge and we'll go partners!

Dentist and Jack E. Leonard

Here's a dental plan. Chew on the other side.

Johnny Barnes, *Sleep When I'm Dead*

DRUGS & ADDICTION

They're selling crack in my neighbourhood. Finally.

Kevin Brennan

Everything I've ever loved was immoral, illegal or grew hair on your palms.

Steve Tyler, frontman of rock band, Aerosmith

Parents that use drugs have kids that use drugs. So there's an important lesson here: don't have kids!

Dave Gold, *The War at Home*

I used to have a drug problem, but now I make enough money.

David Lee Roth

I liked drugs. I was good at them.

Noel Gallagher

Having a wonderful time. Wish I were here.

Carrie Fisher

Taking cocaine is like being a haemophiliac in a razor factory.

Robin Williams

I'm not addicted to cocaine. I just like the way it smells.

Richard Pryor

According to a new report, in England cocaine is cheaper to buy than coffee. So apparently they have Starbucks, too.

Conan O'Brien

Marijuana is self-punishing; it makes you acutely sensitive and, in this world, what worse punishment could there be?

P.J. O'Rourke

She was on Valium and a Sainsbury's wine box a day... She'd lie naked on the kitchen floor at 7 o'clock in the morning, the fridge door open, and the wine box dripping on her head.

Dame Edna Everage

The Bishop of Stortford was talking to the local Master of Hounds about the difficulty he had in keeping his vicars off the incense.

P.G. Wodehouse, *Mr Mulliner Speaking*

Applause is an addiction, like heroin, or checking your email.

Sideshow Mel, *The Simpsons*

They used to tell me, 'Drugs can kill you.' Now that I'm 58, they are saying, 'Drugs can save your life.' I realise my doctor is my dealer now. He's a lot harder to get hold of.

Robin Williams

There were a lot of doctors in rehab. It's rather like being in a fat farm with nutritionists.

Robin Williams

Can you imagine walking through the Priory and seeing Robbie Williams coming over in a dressing gown? That's enough to drive you to heroin.

Noel Gallagher

There are no Chocoholics Anonymous because nobody wants to quit.

Anon

The sun is nature's Prozac.

Astrid Alauda

If you really want a mind-altering experience, look at a tree.

A.C. Grayling

SMOKING

The believing we do something when we do nothing is the first illusion of tobacco.

Ralph Waldo Emerson

I smoke 15 to 20 cigars a day. At my age I need something to hold on to.

George Burns, aged 85

A cigarette was like a little reward I gave myself twenty-five to forty times a day.

Lewis Grizzard

They threaten me with lung cancer, and still I smoke and smoke. If they'd only threaten me with hard work, I might stop.

Mignon McLaughlin

My neighbour asked me for a cigarette. I said, 'I thought you'd stopped smoking.' He said, 'Well, I've managed the first stage – I've stopped buying them.'

Joey Adams

I quit smoking and it was a very, very disappointing experience. I found out my teeth are really brown.

Bill Dana

I gave up smoking four years, two weeks and five days ago. But who misses it?

Sandra Scoppettone

Perfection is such a nuisance that I often regret having cured myself of using tobacco.

Emile Zola

I offered Dawn a cigarette. She refused. 'No thanks, I've already got cancer.'

Elaine Dundy

EDUCATION & THINKING

EDUCATION & SCHOOLS

Free: Mon-Fri: Knowledge. Bring your own containers.

Sign in a school in Dallas, Texas

Isn't education a wonderful thing? If you couldn't sign your name you'd have to pay cash.

Rita Mae Brown

Good news, bad news... I went to 17 different schools in 17 different cities. Good news: I got really good at geography. Bad news: I couldn't spell 'geography'.

Lorna Luft

One of our children's first schools was so posh that when a teacher asked the class, 'Who is Mohammed?' a small boy stuck up his hand and quietly answered, 'Our chauffeur.'

Charles Saatchi, *Charles Saatchi: Question*

The high school I went to, they asked a kid to prove the law of gravity, he threw the teacher out the window.

Thornton Melon, *Back to School*

As for helping me in the outside world, the convent taught me only that if you spit on a pencil eraser, if will erase ink.

Dorothy Parker

A lot of public school boys are twits with polish. When I encounter expensive shirts and upper-class accents I have always presumed vacuity until offered firm evidence to the contrary.

Matthew Parris

I never let my schooling interfere with my education.

Mark Twain

You know there is a problem with the education system when you realize that out of the three Rs only one begins with an R.

Dennis Miller

If we practised medicine like we practise education, we'd look for the liver on the right side and left side in alternate years.

Alfred Kazin

The primary purpose of a liberal education is to make one's mind a pleasant place in which to spend one's time.

Sydney J. Harris

Von Ribbentrop was the new German Ambassador in London, and as a good Nazi, hoped to send his son to Eton.

Peter Ustinov

In my opinion Hook was a good Etonian though not a great one... The proud, if detestable position he attained is another proof that the Etonian is a natural leader of men... In politics he was a Conservative... At Oxford he fell among bad companions – Harrovians.

J.M. Barrie, on his fictional creation, Captain Hook

[*noticing Churchill leave the bathroom without washing his hands*]
—At Eton they taught us to wash our hands after using the toilet.
—At Harrow they taught us not to piss on our hands.

Unidentified Etonian and Winston Churchill, *attrib*.

At Harrow, you could have any boy for a box of Cadbury's milk chocolate.

John Mortimer, an Old Harrovian

There is a certain confidence about anyone who's been to Eton – or to Borstal.

George Passmore, of Gilbert & George

It is a measure of how much the world has changed...that proud Etonians and closet homosexuals have been replaced by proud homosexuals and closet Etonians.

John Julius Norwich, *Trying to Please*

Britain cannot afford a schooling system where the most important book is the cheque book.

Neil Kinnock, on private education

TEACHER

The main purpose of education is to keep them off the streets – the teachers, I mean.

Katharine Whitehorn, quoting her father, a schoolmaster

The secret of teaching is to appear to have known all your life what you learned this afternoon.

Anon

It doesn't matter what you teach a child as long as the child doesn't like it – and does like you.

Collin Brooks

A schoolmaster should have an atmosphere of awe, and walk wonderingly, as if he was amazed at being himself.

Walter Bagehot

Parent-Teacher Night: Let's Share the Blame.

Sign outside Springfield Elementary School,
attended by Bart Simpson, *The Simpsons*

The only reason I always try to meet and know the parents better is because it helps me to forgive the children.

Louis Johannot, teacher

If you promise not to believe everything your child says happens at this school, I'll promise not to believe everything he says happens at home.

Unidentified Schoolteacher

He has glaring faults and they have certainly glared at us this term.

Headmaster's report on Stephen Fry

The boy is every inch the fool, but luckily for him he's not very tall.

School report on Norman Wisdom

I will not yell 'She's dead' during roll call; Global warming did not eat my homework; A burp is not an answer; I am not authorized to fire substitute teachers; Funny noises are not funny; I am not my long-lost twin; I do not have diplomatic immunity; The class hamster isn't 'just sleeping'; I will not hide the teacher's Prozac.

Lines written on the blackboard by Bart Simpson

My teachers told me I would never make anything of myself if I sat staring into space during lessons; however, I had the last laugh as I am now the Astronomer Royal.

Martin Rees, *Viz* magazine

Teaching has ruined more American novelists than drink.

Gore Vidal

One teacher recently retired with $500,000 after 30 years of working hard, caring, dedicating herself and totally immersing herself in the problems of the students. That gave her $50. The rest came from the death of a rich uncle.

Milton Berle

EXAMS & TESTS

Next week I have to take my college aptitude test. In my high school they didn't even *teach* aptitude.

Tony Banta, *Taxi*

Had silicon been a gas, I would have been a major-general by now.

James McNeil Whistler, artist, on being found 'deficient in chemistry' in a West Point exam

English Literature GCSE, Question 1: Discuss the use of imagery and metaphor in *My Story So Far* by Wayne Rooney.
Spell 'Mississippi', without looking at how we've spelt it in the question.
It takes 2 men 10 minutes to check in for their flight – how long will it take Ahmed and Imran?
Thunderbirds are what?

Rejected Exam Questions, *Mock the Week*

I managed to get through the mining exams. They're not very rigorous. They only ask you one question. They say, 'Who are you?' and I got 75 per cent on that.

Peter Cook

Q: The estimated amount of the national debt of England in 1827 is said to have been £900000000; how long would it take to count this debt, supposing you counted $50 per minute, and 12 hours a day, during the whole time? (Sundays excepted.)
A: 354 years, 309 days, 1 hour and 20 mins.

Question from *Conkling's Arithmetic*,
text book of 1831 for children aged 8–10 years

Rufus is a pimp for three girls. If the price is $65 per trick, how many tricks per day must each girl turn to support Rufus' $800 per day crack habit?

Question in a Winnipeg maths exam for
which a teacher was suspended, 2002

COLLEGE

—How do you get a philosophy major off your doorstep?
—Pay for the pizza.

Anon

—Do you think your boy will forget all he learned in college?
—I hope so. He can't make a living drinking.

Larry Wilde

The only thing you study is your navel. You even shave lying down.
Rupert Rigsby, to his student lodger, *Rising Damp*

—He's at Oxford, technically.
—Yes, I met him. Brideshead Regurgitated.

Hannah and Bernard, *Arcadia*

Trinity dons in Hall looking less where they shall sit than where they shall *not* sit.

A.C. Benson

I recollect an acquaintance saying to me that 'the Oriel Common Room stank of Logic'.

John Henry Newman, on the Oxford college

I find the three major administrative problems on a campus are sex for the students, athletics for the alumni, and parking for the faculty.

Clark Kerr

Four years of Harvard College, if successful, resulted in an auto-biographical blank, a mind on which only a watermark had been stamped.

Henry Adams

You want either a first or a fourth. There is no value in anything between.

Evelyn Waugh, *Brideshead Revisited*

INTELLIGENCE

My cat is very intelligent. I asked her what two minus two was and she said nothing.

Brian Johnston

The first time I ever talked to Jonathan Miller his greeting remark was: '*The Times*'s review of my *Tosca* production this morning was disgracefully impertinent – and I use the word in the 17th-century sense.'

Richard Morrison, music critic of *The Times*

He not only overflowed with learning but stood in the slop.

Rev. Sydney Smith, on Thomas Macaulay

When I left the dining room after sitting next to Mr Gladstone, I thought he was the cleverest man in England. But after sitting next to Mr Disraeli, I thought I was the cleverest woman in England.

Princess Marie Louise

Hide your learning, daughter, as if it were a physical defect.

Lady Mary Wortley Montagu

The greatest good you can do for another is not just to share your riches but to reveal to him his own.

Benjamin Disraeli

I am so clever that sometimes I don't understand a single word of what I am saying.

Oscar Wilde

The two biggest myths about me are that I'm an intellectual, because I wear these glasses and that I'm an artist because my films lose money.

Woody Allen

—What do you think of intellectual women?
—Are there any?

Reporter and George Sanders

Educating a beautiful woman is like pouring honey into a fine Swiss watch. Everything stops.

Kurt Vonnegut

A man likes his wife to be just clever enough to appreciate his cleverness, and just stupid enough to admire it.

Israel Zangwill

Diamonds are a girl's best friend. Dogs are a man's best friend. Now you know which sex is smarter.

Nancy Gray

STUPIDITY

It would be easier to pay off the national debt overnight than to neutralise the long-range effects of national stupidity.

Frank Zappa

Think of how stupid the average person is, and then realize half of them are even stupider.

George Carlin

Your brain's so minute that if a hungry cannibal cracked your head open, there wouldn't be enough to cover a small water biscuit.

Edmund Blackadder, *Blackadder*

Think donkey, then take it down a few notches.

David Sedaris

I'll tell you how smart he is. When they had a blackout in New York, he was stranded 13 hours on an escalator.

Joe Nuxhall

Now I may be an idiot, but there's one thing I am not sir, and that sir, is an idiot.

Peter Griffin, *Family Guy*

A man may be a fool and not know it, but not if he is married.

H.L. Mencken

No one can make a man look a fool quite so successfully as a woman. Any man: any woman.

Ray Connolly

—I've changed my mind.
—Yeah, does it work any better?

Bill Barton and Tira (Mae West), *I'm No Angel*

Never call a man a fool. Borrow from him.

Addison Mizner

PHILOSOPHY

—Life is like a bowl of tuna fish.
—Why is life like a bowl of tuna fish?
—How should I know? Am I a philosopher?

Jewish joke

You could read Kant by yourself, if you wanted; but you must share a joke with someone else.

Robert Louis Stevenson

You would not enjoy Nietzsche, Sir. He is fundamentally unsound.
P.G. Wodehouse, *Carry On, Jeeves*

Whenever Westerners don't understand something, they simply think it's Zen.

Yasujiro Ozu

If a tree falls in the forest and nobody is around, the firewood is yours for the taking.

Oleg Vishnepolsky

If a tree falls in a forest and lands on a politician, even if you can't hear the tree or the screams, I'll bet you'd at least hear the applause.
Paul Tindale

It is a safe rule to apply that, when a mathematical or philosophical author writes with a misty profundity, he is talking nonsense.
Alfred North Whitehead

Every professor of philosophy needs a nine-year-old daughter. Mine has a habit of saying, 'Daddy, that is a very silly idea.' She is always right.

A.C. Grayling

I have studied many philosophers and many cats. The wisdom of cats is infinitely superior.

Hippolyte Taine

LIFE, AGEING & DEATH

LIVING

—What happened to you? What's with the bandages and the crutch?
—I was living the life of Riley.
—Then what?
—Riley came home.

Anon

A human lifespan is less than a thousand months long. You need to make some time to think how to live it.

A.C. Grayling

—I've wasted half my life, Marge. Do you know how many memories I have? Three! Standing in line for a movie, having a key made, and sitting here talking to you. Thirty-eight years and that's all I have to show for it.
—You're 39.

Homer and Marge Simpson

Groucho Marx at the end of his life was asked if he had it to do all over again what he would do differently: 'Try another position.'

Gore Vidal

Life is a banquet, and most poor sons-of-bitches are *starving* to death! Live!

Auntie Mame, *Auntie Mame*

—How's life, Mr Peterson?
—Oh, I'm waiting for the movie.

Woody Boyd and Norm Peterson, *Cheers*

I intend to live the first half of my life. I don't care about the rest.

Errol Flynn, who died aged 50

There's more to life than getting drunk, being naked and having sex.

Alex Sibley, *Big Brother 3*

—If you had it all to do over, would you change anything?
—Yes, I wish I had played the black instead of the red at Cannes and Monte Carlo.

Questioner and Winston Churchill

Hope for the best. Expect the worst. Life is a play. We're unrehearsed.

Mel Brooks

AGE & AGEING

First thing I do when I wake up in the morning is breathe on a mirror and hope it fogs.

Early Wynn

My older son who is, I think, here tonight, is 41 years old. Which is odd because so am I.

Robert Parker

Is anyone else here getting older?

Maria Bamford

I am becoming like the Irish Census, I am broken down by age, sex and religion.

Seán MacRéamoinn

I told my wife a man is like wine, he gets better with age. She locked me in the cellar.

Rodney Dangerfield

The first sign of getting old is listening to Radio 2 and thinking it's Radio 1.

Matthew Parris

—You shouldn't let it get to you. You don't look your age.
—Don't I?
—No. You can never tell how old fat people are. The fat pushes the wrinkles out.

Penny Neville and Lindsay Pearce, *Teachers*

I've reached an age where I wake up in the morning, look in the obituary column, and if I don't see my name, I call a hooker.

George Jessel

I recently turned 50, which is young for a tree, midlife for an elephant, and ancient for a quarter-miler, whose son now says, 'Dad, I just can't run the quarter with you anymore unless I bring something to read.'

Bill Cosby

Middle age... the time of a man's life when, if he has two choices for an evening, he takes the one that gets him home earlier.

Alvan L. Barach

Another sign of middle age: questions begin with the words, 'Are you still...'

D.C. Burrows

Middle age was that period of life when parents and children caused equal amounts of worry.

Romy Halliwell

Once you pass 35, your age becomes part of the first sentence of anything written. It's a form of...putting you in your place. For women, naturally. Men still get a free pass, more or less.

Madonna

My wife never lies about her age. She just tells everyone she's as old as I am. Then she lies about *my* age.

Anon

You know you're getting old when... your favourite pastime is surfing the Internet medical sites; the senior citizens in television commercials look 20 years younger than you do; you say, 'Over my dead body!' and people aren't sure if you're kidding.

Joey Green and Alan Corcoran

Nothing makes a woman feel as old as watching the bald spot daily increase on the top of her husband's head.

Helen Rowland

You know you're getting older when by the time you've lit the last candle on your cake, the first one has burned out.

Jeff Rovin

A characteristic of old age is thinking that our own ruin should coincide precisely with that of the universe.

Santiago Ramón y Cajal

An elderly woman in a nursing home declined her pastor's suggestion that she get a hearing aid. 'At 91, I've heard enough,' she said.

Catherine Hall

I did a gig at an old people's home. Tough crowd. They wouldn't respond to my knock-knock jokes until I showed ID.

Frank Skinner

There is no point in growing old unless you can be a witch.

Germaine Greer

A person is always startled when he hears himself seriously called an old man for the first time.

Oliver Wendell Holmes

—You're not the man I knew ten years ago.
—It's not the years, honey, it's the mileage.

Marion Ravenwood and Indiana Jones, *Raiders of the Lost Ark*

I have reached an age when I look just as good standing on my head as I do right side up.

Frank Sullivan

You know when you're really old? When your testicles tell you it's time to mow the lawn.

Rodney Dangerfield

I was actually walking around downtown not too long ago, and I saw Milton Berle in an antique shop – 800 bucks.

Jeffrey Ross, on Milton Berle, aged 87

The older you get, the more important it is not to act your age.

Ashleigh Brilliant

Aztec law... gave the death sentence for all sorts of things – fornication, indignity even – until a man was sixty. Then all the laws were suspended, and he could be as ridiculous as he wanted. I've always wanted to be silly if I felt like it, and now I can.

John Steinbeck, aged 60

I'm not sixty, I'm *sexty*.

Dolly Parton, on reaching the milestone birthday

The great thing about turning 75 is you don't get any more calls from insurance salesmen.

Soupy Sales

—What is the secret of your enduring vigour?
—The saliva of beautiful women.

Interviewer and Tony Curtis, aged 83

I have enjoyed great health at a great age because every day since I can remember, I have consumed a bottle of wine except when I have not felt well. Then I have consumed two bottles.

Bishop of Seville

People are living longer than ever before, a phenomenon undoubtedly made necessary by the 30-year mortgage.

Doug Larson

According to actuarial tables, people who live the longest are rich relatives.

Bob Monkhouse

Death only ever happens to someone ten years older than you, however old you get.

Tim Lott

I think all this talk about age is foolish. Every time I am one year older, everyone else is too.

Gloria Swanson

We are always the same age inside.

Gertrude Stein

Happy Birthday! P.S. If you keep having birthdays, you'll eventually die. Love, Groucho.

Groucho Marx, greetings to a good friend

At whatever age, I hope to die young.

Jean Lemoyne

MEMORY

I remember a lot of things before I was even born. I remember going to a picnic with my father and coming home with my mother.

Foster Brooks

I've a grand memory for forgetting.

Robert Louis Stevenson

To improve your memory, lend people money.

Anon

You are never more than 10 days away from forgetting someone's birthday.

Miles Kington

Women forget injuries but never forget slights.

T.C. Haliburton

Elephants and grandchildren never forget.

Andy Rooney

DEATH & DYING

Think of death as a pie in the face from God.

Tagline, *The End*

—How do you feel about death?
—I don't think it's right for me.

Christopher Howse and Alan Whicker

He's terrified of dying. His theory is that he can't possibly die if he has tickets to the ball game.

George Axelrod, on Irving 'Swifty' Lazar

Dying's not so bad. At least I won't have to answer the telephone.

Rita Mae Brown

Untimely deaths seem common – but I don't remember hearing of a timely one.

Frank A. Clark

I regard it as a matter of honour not to expire before my passport.

Peter Ustinov

The greatest thing about your last journey is that you don't have to pack.

Tony Benn, quoting his grandmother

—I'm settling my estate.
—What estate? Your bus pass and loofah-sponge?

Sophia Petrillo and Dorothy Zbornak, *The Golden Girls*

—Jack is dead.
—Don't be ridiculous. Jack would never die without telling me.

Omar and Joan Wilder, *The Jewel of the Nile*

When they found Michael Jackson lying face down next to the bed they assumed he was looking for the other glove.

Frank Skinner

In an interview, Matthew McConaughey said that he wants to die the same way his father did, right after having sex. McConaughey's mother has said, 'Absolutely not.'

Tina Fey

You don't die in the United States, you underachieve.

Jerzy Kosinski

My Auntie Eileen's getting on a bit now, and she's always going on about who just died: 'D'you remember Arthur? He's just died. D'you remember Mervyn? He's just died.' I said, 'Auntie, get off the roof and give me the gun!'

Milton Jones, *The News Quiz*

The man who invented the taser has passed away at the age of 88. I understand his relatives were stunned.

Conan O'Brien

When a humorist dies, you should go somewhere that has a piano and drink until they throw you out.

Robert Benchley, noted by Alan Coren

I don't like to cross dead people out of my address book. I put them in square brackets.

Julian Barnes

First you are, then you are not. This I find deeply satisfying.

Ingmar Bergman

LAST WORDS

When I was a little kid, I wished the first words I ever said was the word, 'Quote...' so right before I died I could say, '...unquote.'

Steven Wright

When she was dying, she let out a loud fart. 'Good,' she said, looking around her, 'a woman who farts is not dead.' These were the last words she spoke.

Jean-Jacques Rousseau, on the Countess de Vercellis

—If there is anything you'd care to say to me, I shall be only too happy to oblige.
—Much obliged, Padre, but why bother? I'll be seeing your boss in a few minutes.

Minister and Wilson Mizner, on his deathbed

Put out that bloody cigarette!

Saki, to a fellow officer in a trench during World War I, fearing the smoke might give away their positions. A German sniper overheard the remark and shot him.

For Christ's sake, can't you get them to turn off the television!

Bob Brown